TREES
of Los Altos

Camphor Trees on Sylvian Way

TREES
of Los Altos

By Ann Coombs

A pictorial guide to the wide variety of trees that make Los Altos, California, a uniquely beautiful city

TREES of Los Altos a pictorial guide

An earlier edition of this book, edited by Ed Walker, was published in 1970 by the City of Los Altos, California.

Library of Congress Cataloging-in-Publication Data
Coombs, Ann.
Trees of Los Altos: a pictorial guide/Ann Coombs.
ISBN 0-9634623-3-4

Published by Select Books
Copyright 2004, City of Los Altos, California

Printed in U.S.A.

Redwood Grove Park

MANY THANKS TO

Los Altos Environmental Committee
Ken Lim, Chair, Ann Coombs, Hank Cooper,
Jenny Fire-Halvorsen, Judy Fulton, Penny Lave,
Linda DeMichiel, Jocelyn Orr, Julie Saffren

Photography
Ann Coombs (unless otherwise credited)

Consultants
Mary Kaye, Landscape Designer
Daphne Smith, Horticulturalist
Brian McCarthy, City of Los Altos
Paul Nyberg, Publisher

Copy Editor
Elizabeth Robinson

Help locating trees
Susan Moss
Los Altos Garden Club members
Patricia Evans, Landscape Designer
Don McDonald, Historical Commission

Graphics for map
Royston, Hanamoto, Alley & Abey, Landscape Architects
Allyn Feldman, Los Altos History Museum

Grants for printing and distribution
Bob and Marion Grimm
City of Los Altos
Los Altos Community Foundation
Kris Casto

Quercus lobata, VALLEY OAK

TABLE OF CONTENTS

Credits   v
Table of Contents   vi
Introduction   1
Botanical Name Index   2
Common Name Index   3
Tree Photos & Descriptions   4-72
City of Los Altos:
    Design Guidelines for Trees   73
    Street Tree Planting List   73
    Tree Protection Regulations   74
Trees for Under Power Lines: PG&E   75
Trees for Streamsides   75
Trees Resistant to Oak Root Fungus   76
Loving Care of Old Oak Trees   77
Calendar of Flower & Leaf Color   78-79
Trees in Los Altos Civic Center   80-81

INTRODUCTION

Los Altos, a uniquely beautiful city with a mild climate and fertile soil, boasts a wide variety of trees. The Los Altos City Council has recognized the economic and aesthetic values of the diversity of trees in the city. In Resolution 93-8, the council stated, "Trees help stabilize the soil, enhance views, provide privacy, counteract pollutants, maintain the climatic balance, decrease wind velocities, provide shelter for and feed birds and other wildlife, and provide fragrance and color." Trees are very important to the character of the city and add value to individual properties. The whole community benefits when new tree plantings, better care of existing trees, and preservation of old trees occur.

The first edition of *Trees of Los Altos*, authored by Ed Walker, was published in 1970. This 2004 revision contains most of the common trees, including many not in the first book, and a few rare, but spectacular, specimens. There are old venerable heritage trees, remnants of the bountiful orchards that once grew here, such as the apricot orchard surrounding City Hall, and the more recently planted Los Altos signature tree, the Chinese Pistache, that turns brilliant red in the fall. Species that grow happily in Los Altos gardens make up the biggest proportion of this book, but also included are a few "weed" trees that break up paving and readily reseed themselves. For each tree there are addresses where good examples can be seen from the street.

This is not just a pretty book. It is of value to anyone who is choosing trees to plant, or who sees a tree in the book and wants to see the real thing, or who is out walking and spots a particularly interesting tree. Awareness of trees and how they change through the year adds a whole new dimension to walking. There are recommendations for good street trees, trees to plant under power lines, trees resistant to oak root fungus and trees to plant near streams. *Trees of Los Altos* also includes a calendar of colorful flowers and leaves and a map for a tree tour of the Civic Center area, which has many interesting and beautiful trees.

This book is dedicated to all those residents who have planted and cared for trees over the years for all of us to enjoy.

BOTANICAL NAME INDEX

Acacia baileyana	4	Ceratonia siliqua	20	Koelreuteria paniculata	38
Acacia melanoxylon	4	Cercis canadensis	21	Lagerstroemia hybrids	38
Acer buergeranum	5	Cercis occidentalis	21	Laurus nobilis	39
Acer macrophyllum	5	Chamaerops humilis	22	Leptospermum laevigatum	39
Acer palmatum	6	Chitalpa x tashkentensis	22	Ligustrum lucidum	40
Acer palmatum 'Atropurpureum'	6	Cinnamomum camphora	23	Liquidambar styraciflua	40
Acer palmatum 'Sango Kaku'	7	Citrus	23	Liquidambar orientalis	41
Acer platanoides 'Schwedleri'	7	Cornus capitata	24	Liriodendron tulipifera	41
Acer saccharinum	8	Cornus florida	24	Lophostemon confertus*	70
Aesculus californica	8	Crataegus laevigata	25	Lyonothamnus f. asplenifolius	42
Aesculus x carnea	9	Crataegus lavallei*	25	Magnolia (deciduous)	42
Ailanthus altissima	9	Crataegus phaenopyrum	25	Magnolia grandiflora	43
Albizia julibrissin	10	Cupressus arizonica	26	Magnolia liliiflora*	42
Alnus rhombifolia	10	Cupressus sempervirens	26	Malus	43
Araucaria bidwillii	11	Dais cotinifolia	27	Malus 'Robinson'*	43
Araucaria excelsa	11	Diospyros kaki	27	Maytenus boaria	44
Arbutus andrachne 'Marina'	12	Eriobotrya deflexa	28	Melaleuca rhaphiophylla	44
Arbutus menziesii	12	Eriobotrya japonica	28	Melaleuca styphelioides*	44
Arbutus unedo*	12	Erythrina crista-galli	29	Melia azedarach	45
Bambusa or Phyllostachys	13	Eucalyptus ficifolia	29	Metasequoia glyptostroboides	45
Betula jacquemontii	13	Eucalyptus globulus compacta*	30	Morus alba 'Fruitless'	46
Betula nigra	14	Eucalyptus globulus	30	Myoporum laetum	46
Betula pendula	14	Eucalyptus sideroxylon	30	Nyssa sylvatica	47
Brachychiton populneus	15	Fagus sylvatica	31	Olea europaea	47
Braheia armata	15	Ficus carica	31	Parrotia persica	48
Butia capitata	16	Fraxinus a. 'Raywood'*	32	Paulownia tomentosa	48
Callistemon citrinus*	16	Fraxinus uhdei	32	Persea americana	49
Callistemon viminalis	16	Fraxinus velutina 'Modesto'	32	Phoenix canariensis	49
Calocedrus decurrens	17	Geijera parviflora	33	Picea engelmannii	50
Carpinus betulus	17	Ginkgo biloba	33	Picea pungens	50
Castanea dentata	18	Gleditsia triacanthos	34	Pinus canariensis	51
Casuarina equisetifolia	18	Grevillea robusta	34	Pinus eldarica	51
Cedrus atlantica glauca	19	Hymenosporum flavum	35	Pinus mugo mugo	52
Cedrus deodara	19	Ilex aquifolium	35	Pinus pinea	52
Celtis australis*	20	Jacaranda mimosifolia	36	Pinus radiata	53
Celtis sinensis	20	Juglans californica hindsii	36	Pinus thunbergii	53
		Juglans nigra	36	Pistacia chinensis	54
		Juglans regia	37	Pittisporum undulatum	54
		Juniperus chinensis 'Torulosa'	37	Platanus x acerifolia	55
		Koelreuteria bipinnata	38	Platanus racemosa	55

Podocarpus gracilior	56
Podocarpus macrophyllus*	56
Prunus amygdalys	56
Prunus armeniaca	57
Prunus (fruiting plum)	57
Prunus cerasifera	58
Prunus serrulata	58
Prunus serrulata 'Kwanzan'*	58
Pseudotsuga macrocarpa	59
Pseudotsuga menziesii	59
Pyrus calleryana	60
Pyrus kawakamii	60
Quercus agrifolia	61
Quercus douglasii	61
Quercus ilex	62
Quercus lobata	62
Quercus rubra	63
Quercus suber	63
Rhus lancea	64
Robinia pseudoacacia 'Frisia'	64
Robinia x ambigua 'Decaisneana'	65
Robinia x ambigua 'Idahoensis'	65
Salix babylonica	66
Sapium sebiferum	66
Schinus molle	67
Sequoia sempervirens	67
Sequoia sempervirens dwarf*	67
Sequoiadendron giganteum	68
Syagrus romanzoffianum	68
Tamarix	69
Tilia cordata	69
Tristaniopsis l. 'Elegans'	70
Ulmus parvifolia	70
Umbellularia californica	71
Washingtonia robusta	71
Xylosma congestum	72
Zelkova serrata	72

* No photo, see text

COMMON NAME INDEX

Acacia	4
Alder, White	10
Almond	56
Apricot	57
Ash, Evergreen	32
Ash, Modesto	32
Ash, Raywood*	32
Avocado	49
Bamboo	13
Bay Laurel, California	71
Bay, Sweet	39
Beech, Copper	31
Beefwood, Horsetail	18
Birch, Himalayan White	13
Birch, River	14
Birch, Weeping	14
Bottle Brush, Lemon*	16
Bottle Brush, Weeping	16
Bottle Tree	15
Brisbane Box	70
Buckeye, California	8
Bunya Bunya	11
Camphor Tree	23
Carob Tree	20
Cedar, Blue Atlas	19
Cedar, Deodar	19
Cedar, Incense	17
Cherry, Flower. 'Kwanzan'*	58
Cherry, Japanese Flowering	58
Chestnut, American	18
Chestnut, Red Horse	9
China Berry or Honey Tree	45
Chinese Flame Tree	38
Chitalpa	22
Coral Tree	29
Crabapple	43
Crabapple, 'Robinson'*	43
Crape Myrtle	38
Cypress, Arizona	26
Cypress, Italian	26
Dogwood, Eastern	24
Dogwood, Evergreen	24
Elm, Chinese or Evergreen	70
Empress Tree	48
Eucalyptus, Blue Gum	30
Eucalyptus, Pink Ironbark	30
Eucalyptus, Red Gum	29
Eucalypus, Dwarf Blue*	30
Fern Pine	56
Fig, Common	31
Fir, Douglas	59
Golden Rain Tree	38
Hackberry, Chinese	20
Hackberry, European*	20
Hawthorne, Carriere*	25
Hawthorne, English	25
Holly, English	35
Hornbeam	17
Ironwood, Catalina	42
Jacaranda, Sharpleaf	36
Juniper, Twisted Hollywood	37
Laurel, Grecian	39
Lemon	23
Linden Tree	69
Locust, Golden Sunburst	64
Locust, Idaho	65
Locust, Pink	65
Loquat	28
Loquat, Bronze Leaf	28
Madrone	12
Magnolia, Deciduous	42
Magnolia, Chinese	42
Magnolia, Lily*	42
Magnolia, Southern	43
Maidenhair Tree	33
Maple, Big Leaf	5
Maple, Japanese	6
Maple, Japanese (Coral)	7
Maple, Japanese (red-leafed)	6
Maple, Purple Leaf	7
Maple, Silver	8
Maple, Trident	5
Mayten Tree	44
Mimosa	4
Moraine Locust	34
Mulberry, Fruitless	46
Myoporum	46
Norfolk Island Pine	11
Oak, Blue	61
Oak, Coast Live	61
Oak, Cork	63
Oak, Holly	62
Oak, Red	63
Oak, Valley	62
Olive, Common	47
Orange	23
Palm, Canary Island Date	49
Palm, Mexican Blue	15
Palm, Mexican Fan	71
Palm, Pindo	16
Palm, Queen	68
Palm, Windmill	22
Pear, Evergreen	60
Pear, Flowering 'Aristocrat'	60
Pear, Flowering 'Bradford'*	60
Pear, Flower. 'Chanticleer'*	60
Pepper Tree, California	67
Persian Parrotia	48
Persimmon, 'Hachiya'	27
Persimmon, 'Fuyu'*	27
Pine, Canary Island	51
Pine, Eldarica	51
Pine, Italian Stone	52
Pine, Japanese Black	53
Pine, Monterey	53
Pine, Mugho	52
Pistache, Chinese	54
Plane Tree, London	55
Plum, Purple Leaf	58
Plum, fruiting	57
Pompom Tree	27
Podocarpus	56
Prickly Melaleuca	44
Privet, Glossy	40
Redbud, Eastern	21
Redbud, East. 'Forest Pansy'	21
Redbud, Western	21
Redwood, Coast	67
Redwood, Coast, dwarf*	67
Redwood, Dawn	45
Redwood, Giant Sequoia	68
Silk Oak	34
Silk Tree	10
Spruce, Bigcone	59
Spruce, Colorado Blue	50
Spruce, Englemann	50
Strawberry Tree	12
Sumac, African	64
Swamp Paperbark	44
Sweet Gum	40
Sweet Gum, Oriental	41
Sweetshade	35
Sycamore, California	55
Tallow Tree, Chinese	66
Tamarisk	69
Tea Tree, Australian	39
Tree of Heaven	9
Tulip Tree	41
Tulip Tree, Chinese	42
Tupelo	47
Victorian Box	54
Walnut, English	37
Walnut, Black	36
Washington Thorn	25
Willow, Australian	33
Willow, Weeping	66
Xylosma	72
Yew Pine	56
Zelkova, Japanese	72
* No photo, see text.	

3

Acacia baileyana
MIMOSA

This is the evergreen tree with feathery blue-gray foliage, which is a mass of fragrant, yellow puffball flowers in January. Of the many varieties of drought tolerant acacia that grow in Los Altos, this is one of the hardiest. It grows 20-30 feet tall and wide. At the St. Nicholas School on El Monte between Summerhill and Hwy. 280, there are remnants of an old Mimosa orchard, which used to provide mimosa flowers for the New York City flower market. You can see other examples at 1291 and 1225 St. Joseph Ave., and at the entrance to the parking lot for Garden House at Shoup Park on University.

Acacia melanoxylon
BLACKWOOD ACACIA

This is a very common tree in Los Altos, drought tolerant, fast growing, and short lived. It is evergreen with 2-4 inch dull, leathery, green leaves and almost black bark. In March, it is covered with small puffball creamy flowers. It grows to 40 feet tall and 20 feet wide. It has greedy roots and brittle branches. The tree illustrated is at 181 Yerba Santa; another is at the corner of Second and Whitney St.

4

Acer buergeranum
TRIDENT MAPLE

This small, attractive maple has 3 inch, glossy green leaves with only thee lobes. It grows 20-25 feet high and wide and is a good patio tree. Leaves turn red or orange before dropping in the fall. There are three trees in a row at 273 W. Portola.

Acer macrophyllum
BIG LEAF MAPLE

This West Coast native has impressive, 6-15 inch wide pointed-lobe leaves and grows to 30-70 feet tall and 30-50 feet wide. Leaves turn yellow in the fall. Much too big for gardens, you can see it in Redwood Grove on University and next to the outhouse at History House at Hillview Community Center.

Acer palmatum
JAPANESE MAPLE

The Japanese Maple is a tree with artistic branching patterns and small and delicate light green or dark red leaves that turn red before dropping in the fall. It is particularly suitable for small lawns, patios, and for planting in tubs. Its horizontal branching pattern is quite attractive in winter months. Its range of growth is from 10-25 feet. The roots are non-aggressive and resistant to oak root fungus. Some grow best in full sun while others need shade. Examples of this species can be seen at 220 Los Altos Ave., 340 Cherry Ave., 1030 Crooked Creek Dr., 830 Starlite Lane, 88 Yerba Buena, and Shoup Park near Adobe Creek close to Garden House.

Acer palmatum 'Atropurpureum'
RED LEAF JAPANESE MAPLE

A red-leafed variety of Japanese Maple is at 460 Los Altos Ave. The red color is most intense in the sun, fading toward green in the shade. Another red-leafed variety called 'Bloodgood' turns red-orange in the fall.

6

Acer palmatum 'Sango Kaku'
CORAL BARK JAPANESE MAPLE

A variety of Japanese Maple, called 'Sango Kaku,' has coral red branches that are very showy in winter. The leaves are yellow green, turning yellow in the fall. You can see it on the corner of Los Altos and Portola Ave. and at 437 Santa Barbara.

Acer platanoides 'Schwedleri'
PURPLE LEAF MAPLE

Purple leafed varieties of Norway Maple, called 'Schwedleri' (with leaves that turn gold in the fall) and 'Crimson King' (with leaves that stay purple until they drop), are widely planted in Los Altos. These maples grow to 60 feet in height with a spread of up to 50 feet. The wide leaves, with deep lobes and sharp teeth, are easily distinguishable. See examples at 246 Angela Ave. and 108 N. Avalon Dr.

7

Acer saccharinum
SILVER MAPLE

Lacy, five-lobed leaves that are light green above and silvery on the bottom side characterize this maple. It grows fast to 40-100 feet high and wide and should be thinned annually. Its leaves turn a brilliant yellow in fall before dropping. The bark is gray and smooth when young and turns to reddish brown and flakes with age. Roots can be a problem. It has brittle branches that break easily and suffers from aphids and scale. The one pictured is on Angela near Cielito. There is another at 1979 Kent.

Aesculus californica
CALIFORNIA BUCKEYE

The striking candleabra of fragrant white flower plumes in late spring characterize this tree, and the hummingbirds love it. It is native to the California Coast Range, where it usually loses its leaves in July, but under garden watering conditions it leafs out in January and keeps its leaves until fall. The leaves are made up of five to seven leaflets each 3-5 inches long. Buckeye has shiny golf ball size seeds. Wider than tall, it grows to 20 feet high and 30 feet wide. The specimen pictured is at 620 Lincoln. Others are at 11 Cypress Ct. and on the corner of Portland and Miramonte Ave.

8

Aesculus x carnea
RED HORSE CHESTNUT

In spring, this small deciduous tree is covered with plumes of red or pink flowers that attract hummingbirds. The leaves are large and dark green, divided into five leaflets. It grows to 30 feet high and 25 feet wide. The one pictured is at the corner of Russell and Covington. Another can be found at 755 Alvinia and there are several on Main and on State St., mixed in with the Chinese Pistache trees.

Ailanthus altissima
TREE OF HEAVEN

This is a deciduous, rapid growing, invasive, weed tree with luxuriant compound leaves, 1-3 feet long. It is extremely hardy and grows where other trees will not survive. Male trees, with their smelly flowers, should not be planted, for fertilized seeds reproduce rapidly and make it quite difficult to control proliferation. Female trees have spectacular clusters of rusty brown or yellow winged seedpods. The specimen pictured is at 900 Santa Rita Ave. Another is on the parking lot side of 50 Fourth St.

9

Albizia julibrissin
SILK TREE

This beautiful deciduous tree with light-sensitive, finely divided, feathery leaves that fold up at night, boasts masses of fluffy pink or salmon colored flowers in July. Its flat top, spreading wider than it is tall, is especially nice to look at from above. The flowers are attractive to birds. Dropping flowers, leaves and seedpods can be quite messy. Nice examples are located at 37 Portola, 295 Los Altos Ave., 2391 Montclaire, 1664 Newcastle, and the corner of E. Edith and Gordon.

Alnus rhombifolia
WHITE ALDER

This fast growing native deciduous tree loves water. It has smooth light gray bark and sharply toothed leaves with edges that curl under. The leaves are dark green above and light green underneath. The tiny cones that hang on through the winter are very distinctive. It grows quickly to 50-90 feet tall and 40 feet wide. The pictured tree is at 1054 Highland Circle. There are also some in one courtyard of the Hillview Community Center. At 55 North Gordon see **Alnus cordata**, Italian Alder, with 1 inch cones.

10

Araucaria bidwillii
BUNYA BUNYA

This 80 foot tall giant evergreen conifer from Australia is a sight to be seen. It has spiny overlapping leaves and giant cones. The pictured tree is in an island in the middle of Middlebury Lane.

Araucaria excelsa
NORFOLK ISLAND PINE

This tree is an evergreen with a very symmetrical branching system. Its well-proportioned branches spread out horizontally and are covered with bright green, needle-like leaves. Big old Norfolk Island Pines in Los Altos seem to have succumbed to frost. Young specimens make excellent tub trees and can be used as indoor plants. It also makes a fine lawn tree. It can grow to 100 feet tall and 60 feet wide. There is a young specimen at the northeast corner of the main library.

Arbutus menziesii
PACIFIC MADRONE

This California native evergreen is distinguishable by its beautifully polished twigs, peeling red bark, and dark green leathery 3-6 inch leaves. In March it has greenish-white flowers reminiscent of lily of the valley. In the fall it has clusters of orange-red berries in profusion. It often grows into picturesque shapes with twisted trunk and branches, and its height is unpredictable. This tree is fussy about growing conditions and is difficult to establish. A specimen can be seen at 634 Jay St., and it is often seen in the Coastal Range.

Arbutus unedo and
A. andrachne 'Marina'
STRAWBERRY TREE

This is a beautiful, small evergreen tree with twisty, knotted branches, shredding reddish-brown bark and dark green, 3 inch, leathery leaves. Blooming in October and November, the lily of the valley-like flowers can be white or pink. The bright red, but often mealy, edible fruit looks like strawberries and can be messy. The tree grows to 8-30 feet high and wide. PG&E recommends it as a tree to plant under power lines. The white-flowered variety can be found at 430 Guadalupe Dr., 581 Jay St., and 271 Silvia Court. Pink flowered Arbutus andrachne 'Marina' is at the northeast corner of Cuesta and El Monte.

Bamboo family: Phyllostachys aurea ⇩
GOLDEN BAMBOO

There are several varieties of the Bamboo family in this area used very effectively for hedges and as screens. Golden Bamboo grows 2 inch diameter yellowish culms 10-20 feet tall. Running bamboos must be confined with a 30 inch deep metal barrier or they will take over your garden and house foundation. The pictured bamboo is at 543 Cherry Ave. Another is at 637 Stardust Lane. Clumping Bamboos can be easily contained and respond well to clipping and trimming. Good types are Bambusa multiplex Alphonse Karr (8-10 feet tall), Bambusa oldhamii (15-25 feet tall) and Otatea acuminata aztecorum (8-20 feet tall which can be seen in front of History House).

Betula jacquemontii
HIMALAYAN
WHITE BIRCH

Beautiful Betula jacquemontii has exceptionally brilliant white bark and a pyramidal shape. It needs regular water and grows fast, reaching about 40 feet high and 20-30 feet wide. Leaves turn yellow in the fall. Examples can be seen at 451 Carmel, 53 Alma, 25 N. Avalon, and at the corner of San Antonio Road and Parson's Way.

13

Betula nigra
RIVER BIRCH

River birch has fewer problems than other birches. It has shiny pinkish bark and glossy green, diamond-shaped leaves with somewhat silvery undersides. It grows quickly to 50 feet high and 40 feet wide. Leaves turn yellow in the fall. Several examples planted in clusters are at 321 N. Clark.

Betula pendula
EUROPEAN OR WEEPING
WHITE BIRCH

These beautiful deciduous trees are widely planted in Los Altos and provide yellow leaves for fall color. They require regular watering and are susceptible to aphids, which drip sticky honeydew, making a black mess on patios. These birch trees are fast growing to 30-60 feet tall and 20-40 feet wide. Good examples of Weeping Birch can be found at the southeast corner of Edith and Third St. and at 34 N. Avalon Dr.

14

Brachychiton populneus
BOTTLE TREE

This evergreen tree has a bottle-shaped trunk that bulges at the bottom and rises to a conical crown. Its bright green leaves resemble those of a poplar. It is a dense, erect, and symmetrical tree that grows to a maximum of approximately 60 feet with a spread of about 40 feet. It flowers in May or June with 1/2 inch white bell-shaped blossoms followed by woody, canoe-shaped seed-pods. It is a slow grower, drought tolerant and resistant to pests and disease, but frost sensitive. Specimens can be seen at 625 Milverton and 1734 Hawkins.

Braheia armata
MEXICAN BLUE PALM

This palm has silvery blue, almost white fan-shaped leaves and showy creamy hanging clusters of flowers in July. It grows slowly to 20-40 feet tall with a 12 foot spread. This is one of the lesser known palms, and it is one well worth considering if you like a tropical setting. This specimen is at 2059 Kent. There is also one at 1865 Alford Ave.

15

Butia capitata
BLUE PINDO PALM

This beautiful palm grows slowly to 20 feet tall with leaves spreading 10-15 feet wide. It has feathery blue-gray fronds and long spikes of creamy flowers followed by edible fruits. The pictured tree is at 99 Sylvian Way.

Callistemon viminalis
WEEPING BOTTLE BRUSH

This drought tolerant evergreen tree with weeping branches grows to a height of 20-30 feet with a spread of about 15 feet. Its narrow, 3 inch long leaves are soft, light green with bronze tips. Bright red bottlebrush shaped flowers, appearing in May through October, attract bees and hummingbirds. A specimen is at 366 S. El Monte. **Callistemon citrinus**, Lemon Bottle Brush, is a fast-growing evergreen shrub or small tree that grows to 10-15 feet high and about 10 feet wide. It has soft, green foliage and bright red flowers in the summertime, attracting bees and hummingbirds. It needs monthly irrigation. Specimens may be seen at 655 Almond Ave., 385 Anita, and along Foothill Blvd. near Cristo Rey Dr.

16

Calocedrus decurrens
INCENSE CEDAR

This native evergreen is a dense, columnar tree that can grow from 50-150 feet in height with a spread of 12-50 feet. Its pendulous branches have flat sprays of bright green to yellowish leaves, which give off a fragrance when crushed. The bark is rich red-brown and the cones are small. It is drought tolerant. Specimens can be seen at 1824 Farndon, 109 Lyell St., 611 Palm, the corner of Cielito and Galli, and at 156 Los Altos Ave.

Carpinus betulus 'fastigiata'
HORNBEAM

Dark green sawtooth-edged leaves, which hang on late in the year and gray bark characterize this deciduous tree. It can be single or multi-trunk and grows to 40 feet high. It has a nice root system, making it a good tree to garden under. The pictured specimen is at 26 N. Avalon Drive.

Castanea dentata
AMERICAN CHESTNUT

This is the great American tree that has been decimated in large areas of the country by a blight for which no cure has been found. The tree is deciduous with pendulous light-green leaves, long sprays of white flowers in June, and a fruit which is a prickly burr containing an edible nut. It grows to a maximum of 100 feet with a great spread of from 70-100 feet. The bark is grayish brown. A similar looking tree is **Castanea sativa**, European Chestnut. Examples of Chestnuts can be seen at 1097 N. Clark, 2090 Crist Dr., 87 Lyell Street, and 24 Del Monte.

Casuarina
equisetifolia
HORSETAIL
BEEFWOOD

This evergreen is a narrow, upright-growing tree with slender, graceful branches. It has needle-like twiglets with inconspicuous leaves, and it gives the appearance of a pine tree. Its delicate look belies its rugged character, for it is drought resistant, strong growing, and takes little attention. It grows to 40-70 feet with a spread of about 20-35 feet. This tree is recommended by Los Altos as a good street tree for a large space. It may be seen at the following locations: 355 Cuesta, 755 Alvina, and 250 S. Gordon.

18

Cedrus atlantica glauca
BLUE ATLAS CEDAR

This beautiful evergreen is distinguishable by its open growth patterns, the formal arrangement of its branches, and its blue-green needles that grow in small tufts. It is a large tree ranging from 30-100 feet in height with a spread of 30-60 feet. When young it looks fragile and is often planted with little thought for its eventual size. Thus it often overpowers a small garden. There are many in Los Altos, especially near the older historical houses. See it at 220 University, 546 Orange, and 461 Hacienda.

Cedrus deodara
DEODAR CEDAR

This evergreen (native to the Himalayas) is a graceful, beautiful tree with wide-spreading branches that droop at the tips. It is deep rooted and drought tolerant. It grows to heights of from 50-100 feet with a spread up to 60 feet. Thus it should be used only in large gardens and should be planted alone. The soft needles are green, yellow green, or bluish green, in small tufts. The cones are from 3-5 inches in length and shatter when they fall, leaving an upright spike on the branch. There are many mature Deodar trees in the Los Altos area. The one pictured is at 384 Verano. See it also at 1220 Berry, 725 University, and the corner of Rinconada Way and El Monte Ave.

Celtis australis and Celtis sinensis
HACKBERRY

⇩

Similar to elms, but smaller, these deciduous trees have the advantage that they never send out shallow roots that can destroy paving. They have small fruits that attract birds. Hackberry is recommended as a good street tree by the city of Los Altos. C. australis grows to 50-80 feet and 30 feet wide. See it at 615 Milverton. The pictured C. sinensis, Chinese Hackberry, grows only to 50 feet tall and wide. It can be seen in the Almond School parking lot.

⇨

Ceratonia siliqua
CAROB TREE

A broad-leaved evergreen tree, this specimen is highly adaptable to garden use, is very ornamental, and provides deep shade. It is a round, compact tree with clean, shiny, dark green, compound leaves and long narrow seedpods of chocolate-tasting beans with high nutritional value. It grows from 20-50 feet in height with a spread of an equal size. In spring, red buds open into small yellowish blossoms. Carob is on the list of Los Altos recommended street trees. It is resistant to oak root fungus. Specimens may be seen at 1022 Golden Way, opposite 60 Ceilito, at 5150 El Camino, and as a street tree on both Carob Lane and Sherman Street.

20

Cercis canadensis
EASTERN REDBUD

This small deciduous round-headed tree, native to the East Coast of the United States, grows to 25 feet high and wide. It is covered with tiny sweetpea-shaped flowers, white to cerise, in late March. The leaves are round and 3-4 inches in diameter. Variety 'Forest Pansy' has pink flowers and purple leaves. Varieties 'Alba' and 'Texas' have white flowers. All varieties will have fall color, usually yellow. Redbud is on the Los Altos recommended street tree list and on PG&E's list of trees to plant under power lines. Specimens can be seen at 375 Yerba Buena, 1050 Covington, and on the corner of Miramonte and Stanley Ave. Variety 'Forest Pansy' is at 679 and 746 University.

Cercis occidentalis
WESTERN REDBUD

This Redbud is native to California. It is a slow growing, deciduous tree 10-20 feet tall with the same spread. It looks brushy with several trunks from the base. In the early spring it is covered with small, lavender-red, sweetpea-shaped flowers and is rather spectacular. In the fall, the round, 4 inch, blue-green leaves turn yellow or bright red. In wintertime its bare branches are covered with clusters of reddish-brown seedpods. It is drought tolerant and resistant to oak root fungus. See at 868 Altos Oaks Ave., 264 Portola Ave. and the History Museum at Hillview Community Center.

21

Chamaerops humilis
WINDMILL PALM

This small, exotic-looking palm comes from the western Mediterranean. Its slender trunk is covered with woody remnants of old leaf stems and stringy black fibers. Multiple trunks thicken gradually as they rise to the crown of lacy fan-shaped leaves. It is useful on a patio, as a tub specimen. It grows between 10-30 feet in height. This is the most frost tolerant of the palms. See specimens at 10 Angela and 1990 Kent.

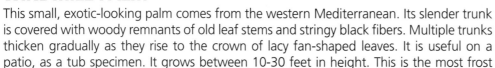

Chitalpa x
tashkentensis
CHITALPA

Big clusters of frilly, white or pink or lavender flowers from late spring through fall characterize this tree. It is fast growing to 20 or 30 feet tall and wide. Leaves are 1 inch wide and 5 inches long. This tree is deciduous and drought tolerant and easy to live with. Chitalpa is a cross between catalpa and chilopsis linearis. See it at 49 Lyell, 1510 Oak, and 653 University.

Cinnamomum camphora
CAMPHOR TREE

This broad-leaved evergreen is a wide-spreading, dense tree that provides deep, heavy shade. Its yellow-green leaves take on a bronze cast in winter and new growth is reddish. Although the roots tend to surface unless deep watered and may invade sewers, Camphor is on the Los Altos list of recommended street trees for large spaces. The leaves smell of camphor when crushed. Camphor trees grow slowly to 40-50 feet in height and a spread of about 30-60 feet. Camphor is susceptible to oak root fungus. There are many examples in Los Altos. Look at the street trees on Sylvian Way and on Hawthorne from El Monte to Clark. This photo was taken at 400 E. Edith.

Citrus: ORANGE and LEMON

Citrus trees are very decorative in the landscape with their dark, lustrous, evergreen leaves, sweet-smelling flowers, and colorful fruit. They need good drainage, regular water and lots of fertilizer. Grafted onto dwarf rootstock, they grow to 15 feet high and wide. Their branches are armed with sharp spines. 'Valencia' oranges mature in summer and store well on the tree, getting sweeter all the time. The seedless 'Washington Navel' oranges have fruit that ripens in midwinter. See nice orange trees at 888 Stagi, 659 Jay St., and the corner of E. Edith and Sunkist. 'Eureka' Lemon produces tasty fruit at lower summer temperatures than other citrus. See it at 1570 Wakefield, 24 Marvin, 220 E. Edith, and on the corner of East Edith and Sunkist.

Cornus capitata
EVERGREEN DOGWOOD

This dogwood grows 20-30 feet tall and wide. The inconspicuous flowers are surrounded by 2 inch wide creamy white bracts, putting on a big show in late spring. They are followed by large strawberry-colored fruits, showy but messy. The gray green leaves turn purplish in the fall. See this special tree at 732 University.

Cornus florida
EASTERN
DOGWOOD

This deciduous dogwood, native to the eastern United States, has beautiful horizontal branches and, in springtime, inconspicuous flowers surrounded by large creamy or pink bracts. It grows to 20-30 feet high and wide and has clusters of small red fruits that attract birds. It is subject to a lot of diseases, but has recently been crossbred with Kousa Dogwood to produce somewhat disease-resistant hybrids. There is a nice Eastern Dogwood growing at 868 Altos Oaks Drive.

24

Crataegus laevigata
HAWTHORN

Deciduous Hawthorn trees are known for white or pink flowers in late spring, 2 inch lobed leaves, and red berries that hang on into winter. They need fairly austere conditions, sun and moderate water. Bees and birds love them. They are subject to fire blight. Some examples of Crataegus laevigata, with pink flowers, can be seen at History House, 104 Alvarado, 745 University, 315 Alta Vista, and 370 Yerba Buena. **Crataegus lavallei** or Carriere Hawthorn, taller than other hawthorns, has dark green, leathery, toothed leaves and 3/4 inch red berries. See it at 371 Cherry and 720 University. Crataegus trees are recommended by PG&E as a tree to plant under power lines.

Crataegus phaenopyrum
WASHINGTON THORN

Washington Thorn is a graceful deciduous tree which is interesting in all seasons. It has clusters of small white flowers in late spring, lobed green leaves that turn red in the fall, and clusters of bright red berries in fall and winter. Its branches have long thorns. It grows moderately fast to 25 feet with a 20 foot spread. See it at 618 Sheridan, and 770 University.

Cupressus arizonica
ARIZONA CYPRESS

This conifer is drought tolerant and will attain a height of 20-40 feet, and a width of 8-30 feet. The young trees have blue-green foliage that turns to gray-green as the tree matures. Cones are the size of golf balls and shaped with overlapping plates. On older trees, the bark is gray and craggy. Specimens can be seen at 881 Berry, 497 University, at the corner of Monterey and Cypress and in downtown Los Altos Parking Plaza North (on the north side between Second and Third streets).

Cupressus sempervirens
ITALIAN CYPRESS

This tree is easily distinguished by its tall, narrow shape and full foliage of scale-like dark green needles. The species is very often used in formal borders to accent vertical lines. It develops to a height of 60 feet with a spread of about 8-12 feet. The tree requires very little care. It should not get too much water, nor should it be planted in very fertile soil. See specimens along Cypress Drive, at 230 and 239 El Monte, 300 Marich, 894 University, and 338 Verano.

26

Dais continifolia
POMPOM TREE

This is a small deciduous tree or large shrub that has soft, green foliage and seldom grows to more than 20 feet in height. In mid-summer it is covered with bright-pink flowers that are in evidence for over a month. It is easy to grow, needing only the average amount of maintenance, and is very drought resistant. Specimens can be seen in the North Parking Plaza between Third and Fourth Streets.

Diospyros kaki
ORIENTAL PERSIMMON

The persimmon is a deciduous tree with brilliant orange-red edible fruit that hangs on the tree even after the leaves have turned from green to fiery red and have dropped from the branches. A handsome tree, it grows to a height of between 20 and 40 feet with an equal spread. There are two varieties: 'Hachiya' has round slightly pointed fruit that must be very ripe and mushy before eating or it will pucker your mouth. See it at 41 and 215 Hawthorne, 175 Galli, and the corner of Covington and Echo. Non-astringent 'Fuyu' has flat fruit that is very sweet and should be eaten crisp like an apple. The leaves turn a soft apricot color in the fall. See it in Shoup Park to the left of Garden House.

27

Eriobotrya deflexa
BRONZE-LEAFED LOQUAT

This broadleaf evergreen is a smaller, copper or bronze leafed variety of loquat. It has showy, white, spring flower clusters and no edible fruit. The leaves are shinier and smaller than those of fruiting loquat. It can be seen at 531 Clark and 1560 Oak.

Eriobotrya
japonica
LOQUAT

The loquat is a handsome tree that grows into a symmetrical shape and attains a height of between 15 and 30 feet with equal spread. Its leaves are large, dark green, and tropical appearing, dark green above and wooly, reddish brown beneath. It is an evergreen and needs only moderate water. Dull white flower clusters appear in winter. The yellow-orange fruit, which ripens in April, grows in clusters of from three to ten pear-shaped, 1-2 inches long fruit. The taste is tart, but the fruit makes excellent preserves. It grows so abundantly that pruning to shape is necessary. Some examples to see are at 1225 Eva, 1305 Oak, 531 Hawthorne, and 1194 Thurston.

28

Erythrina crista-galli
CORAL TREE

This is a medium-sized tree or a large shrub, which should be protected from frost damage. It grows to about 15 feet in height and develops about the same spread. It is deciduous with shiny green fan-like leaves that are divided into three leaflets. Very showy red flowers clustered on long stems appear in spring, summer and late fall. It is resistant to oak root fungus. The seeds are poisonous if eaten. See specimens at 1969 Kent Drive and behind History House in the Civic Center.

Eucalyptus ficifolia
RED FLOWERING GUM

This compact, round-headed eucalyptus has leathery leaves, dark green above and pale below. It has showy clusters of red or orange to red flowers in August. Choose this plant when it is in bloom to get the color you like. It grows 18-30 feet tall. Good in a dry part of the garden, it will not grow well in a lawn. Good examples are at 154 Almond Ave. and 560 El Monte.

29

Eucalyptus globulus
BLUE GUM

These are huge messy trees, 200 feet high and 40 to 60 feet wide. Leaves on young shoots are grey-blue and almost round. Older leaves are slender and long. The bark peels off the tree in strips. The tree litters bark, leaves, seedpods, and brittle branches. The roots invade sewers and break sidewalks. Big Blue Gums can be seen next to the Chamber of Commerce building at Foothill Expressway and Main Street and on El Monte Ave. **Eucalyptus globulus compacta**, Dwarf Blue Gum, is much smaller. It grows to about 30 feet high and 15 feet wide. It is bushier, better shaped, but just as messy and voracious. There are plantings on Foothill Expressway, El Monte Road, and on Fremont Avenue between Loyola Corners and Sunnyvale.

Eucalyptus sideroxylon
PINK IRONBARK

This eucalyptus has furrowed red-brown bark, blue-green leaves, and showy pink flowers in the winter. It grows 40-80 feet tall and should be pruned to prevent brittle limbs from breaking off. There are specimens at the Fire Station on Almond, 761 University, and in the parking lot behind 4920 El Camino. It is a street tree on Arboretum, and also on Grant between Covington and Bryant.

Fagus sylvatica 'Atropunicea'
COPPER BEECH

This handsome deciduous tree with bronze foliage holds its leaves late in the year and has an attractive lacy branching pattern in winter. However, it needs lots of water and forms dense mats of shallow roots, which interfere with growing grass or a garden beneath. It grows to 50 feet. Specimens can be seen at 905 Golden Way, 1168 Russell, and 896 Stagi.

Ficus carica
COMMON FIG

This is a picturesque tree with wide spreading branches that form a rounded crown. It is deciduous with tropical-looking dark green leaves that turn yellow in the fall. The trunk is often formed in multiples and the bark is smooth and dark gray. The tree bears fruit when three years old. Fig trees grow 15-30 high and wide. It is best to keep the tree pruned low enough to make picking figs easy, otherwise dropping fruit can be a problem. The recommended pruning time is during the winter or early spring. See it at 805 and 817 Berry, 985 Campbell, 180 Hillview Ave, 1232 Golden Way, 275 Valley St., and the vacant lot at University Ave. and Quinnhill.

Fraxinus uhdei
EVERGREEN ASH

This tree is either deciduous or evergreen depending upon the climate. In this area mature trees keep their leaves the year round. The tree grows quickly to 40 feet in height with a spread of 15-20 feet or more. Its bright green, 18-inch long leaves are divided into leaflets. The branches can be brittle. See specimens at 1457 Morton, 1785 Newcastle and an enormous old one in an island on Longdon Circle.

Fraxinus augustifolia 'Raywood,' Raywood Ash, is a rapid growing, oval, upright tree to 40 feet tall. Leaves, smaller and more delicate-looking than other ashes, turn claret red in the fall. Seedless and resistant to common ash problems, Raywood Ash is recommended by the City of Los Altos for street tree planting. There are two at 763 Parma.

Fraxinus velutina 'Modesto'
MODESTO ASH

This ash variety has smooth leaves, smooth bark, and light green foliage. It grows 50 feet high and 30 feet wide. Trees of the ash species are very durable. In the fall, their bright yellow leaves add a dash of color to the landscape. Modesto Ash is subject to a fungus called anthracnose that causes the new spring leaves to drop off in wet weather. However, the trees soon recover and provide shade all summer. Modesto Ash can be seen in the parking lot at Hillview Community Center. It is also commonly planted as a street tree in the area north of Fremont Avenue and east of El Monte Road. This photo was taken on Santa Barbara where the branches make a canopy over the road.

Geijera parviflora
AUSTRALIAN WILLOW

This is a lovely, medium-sized evergreen tree from Australia that has weeping branches. Its dull-green leaves are 3-6 inches long and thin. It is a slow-growing tree achieving heights of about 25-35 feet with an almost equal spread. The roots are deep and non-invasive and it is drought resistant. It requires no special care. This tree is recommended by the City of Los Altos as a good medium sized, evergreen street tree if root barriers are used. Examples of this species can be seen at 1724 Oak and 898 Stagi.

Ginko biloba
MAIDENHAIR TREE

This exotic conifer, a survivor from prehistoric times, was imported originally from China. It is a slender-branched, lacy tree that attains a height of 50-80 feet and width of 25-40 feet. It requires moderate water and is resistant to oak root fungus. The fan-shaped leaves are a delicate green and turn brilliant yellow before dropping. Be sure to plant only male trees, because female trees drop many very smelly fruits. See at 654 Orange Avenue, 40 and 48 S. Avalon Dr., and as a street tree on Azalea.

33

Gleditsia triacanthos
MORAINE LOCUST

This is a wide-spreading, symmetrical tree with bright green, fern-like leaves that are attached to long stems. Pale flowers yield seedpods 12-18 inches long. In the fall this deciduous tree turns a clear yellow. It can grow to a height ranging from 25-75 feet with a spread of 35 feet, so it needs plenty of room. It requires no special attention, but is subject to wind breakage. It has a long dormancy period. When buying, specify the thornless variety. See specimens at 675 Orange Avenue, 636 Palm Ave, and next to the Senior Center at Hillview. (Compare with Robinia pseudoacacia 'Frisia'.)

Grevillea robusta
SILK OAK

This drought tolerant evergreen is a narrow tree growing in many shapes up to 70 feet with a spread of 10-35 feet. Its foliage is dark green and feathery. Its summertime blooms of orange flowers appear in showy slender sprays. This is a weed tree, messy and with invasive roots. Keep it in outlying areas. Brittle branches are subject to wind damage. It can be seen at 661 Clark near El Monte, 1891 Farndon, and in an island on Austin near Juarez.

34

Hymenosporum flavum
SWEETSHADE

This graceful, broadleaf evergreen is native to Australia. The 4-6 inch long leaves are narrow, glossy and dark green. Perfumed flowers in early summer are soft yellow and very showy. The tree has a very open growth pattern and needs frequent pinching when young to encourage a stronger plant. Growing at a moderate rate, it reaches 40 feet tall and 20 feet wide. It can be seen at 299 Marich and in the alley behind 144 Giffin.

Ilex aquifolium
ENGLISH OR DUTCH HOLLY

This is the holly tree that provides holly sprigs with red berries for Christmas decorations. It is a slow growing evergreen with the familiar dark green, shiny leaves with spiny edges. There is also a variegated variety. Female trees bear the berries; male trees do not. The tree forms a dense and narrow pyramid. It will grow to a height of 20-40 feet as a tree and is resistant to oak root fungus. Specimens are to be seen at 246 Hillview Ave., 561 Orange, and 398 University.

35

Jacaranda mimosifolia
SHARPLEAF JACARANDA

This deciduous tree with its delicate-looking foliage is green in mild winters and loses its leaves just before blooming in late spring. It requires pruning for good shaping and will die back in severe frosts and grow again from the roots. In late spring and summer, long showy clusters of brilliant lavender-blue flowers bloom in profusion. The seedpods look like 2 inch castanets and are popular with floral designers. It grows from 25-60 feet tall with a medium spread. It is resistant to oak root fungus. See specimens at 781 Berry, 1725 Granger, 586 Orange and 1253 Thurston.

Juglans californica hindsii and J. nigra
BLACK WALNUT

These members of the walnut family grow to about 40-100 feet in height and spread almost as wide. The one called Juglans nigra becomes somewhat ragged with age. The California native, Juglans californica hindsii, is distinguished for its high branching habit and smooth surface on the nut. Both are deciduous and have large leaves that are divided into many 3-5 inch long leaflets. The bark is dark and craggy. They are drought tolerant and resistant to oak root fungus, but hard to garden under. Don't plant them near a creek. Both trees have been used as street trees in Los Altos. See specimens at 1030 and 1146 Miramonte, and in the center divide of Fremont near Newcastle.

Juglans regia
ENGLISH WALNUT

English walnuts have dark brown, edible nuts that are much milder in flavor than those of black walnut. The deciduous tree grows to 60 feet high and wide. Its leaves are bright green, have 5-7 leaflets, and the individual leaflets are broader than black walnut. The bark is smooth and silvery gray. Juglans regia is usually grafted onto Juglans hindsii rootstock, and you can see the graft line on the trunk. It is hard to garden under and has leaves that readily stain clothes dark brown. English Walnut specimens are seen at 817 Berry, at 1295 Fremont, on the corner of Golden Way and Altos Oaks, on Lyell near Gabilan, and on University near Shoup Park. This photo was taken at 1390 Miramonte.

Juniperus chinensis 'Torulosa'
TWISTED or HOLLYWOOD JUNIPER

This variety can be used as an accent plant in the garden or in tubs. It is an erect tree with twisted branches that give it a picturesque shape. Rich green in color, the overlapping scales of the foliage give the branches a braided look. It can grow to a height of 20 feet. It is subject to root rot from over-watering and die back from juniper blight. Specimens can be seen at 76 Alma Ct., 675 Berry, 664 Jay, 398 Yerba Buena, and at 1550 Siesta.

37

Koelreuteria paniculata and bipinnata
GOLDEN RAIN TREE

These deciduous trees are recommended by the City of Los Altos as street trees. They grow to 25-35 feet tall and wide and have deep roots. The leaves are 1-2 feet long with many oval leaflets. K. paniculata has showy clusters of yellow flowers in early summer followed by red Chinese-lantern shaped seed capsules which turn brown. The other variety, K. bipinnata, blooms in late summer and has 2 inch lantern-shaped seed capsules that are orange or red into the fall. Both varieties need moderate water. Specimens of K. paniculata can be seen at 188 Alvaredo, 5150 El Camino, 586 El Monte, and 757 University.

Lagerstroemia hybrids
CRAPE MYRTLE

This is a beautiful deciduous tree with dark green leaves that turn red and gold in the fall. Showy blossom clusters are white, pink, red, or purple, depending on the variety. It has a long dormant period but the trunk and branches are beautifully polished in winter when the smooth bark peels off. It grows from 10-25 feet high and needs pruning for shape. After tree growth is formed, it should be pruned annually for best flowering. Choose new varieties that are resistant to mildew. Recommended by Los Altos as a small street tree and by PG&E as a tree to plant under power lines. See specimens at 37 N. Avalon Dr., 51 Angela, 393 N. Clark, 132 Yerba Santa, and the Costume Bank on State and Third St.

Laurus nobilis
GRECIAN LAUREL OR SWEET BAY

This is the historic tree of poets and scholars of ancient Greece. It is evergreen and grows slowly with a multiple trunk to a perfectly round shape with dense, dark-green oval foliage 2-4 inches long. (California Bay Laurel leaves are narrower.) It reaches between 12 and 40 feet high and wide, but can be well controlled by pruning. The leaves are used for seasoning. Oil extracted from its purple berries is used to make perfume. It suckers readily and needs good drainage. This tree can be seen at 315 Portola.

Leptospermum laevigatum
AUSTRALIAN TEA TREE

This is an evergreen with a long history. Legend has it that Captain Cook cured his crew of scurvy with a tea made from its leaves. Gray-green leaves accent the gray shaggy bark, and the trunk and branches twist into fantastic shapes. There are half inch white flowers in April. As a tree it will grow to 30 feet in height. As a shrub a growth of 10-15 feet is common. It needs good drainage and slightly acid soil. The specimen shown is at the Chamber of Commerce, 321 University.

39

Ligustrum lucidum
GLOSSY PRIVET

This is a drought resistant, round headed, evergreen tree that grows 20-40 feet tall with equal spread. It has 3-5 inch glossy green leaves and large clusters of small white flowers in summer. It has been widely planted in Los Altos as a street tree but has many disadvantages. The flowers produce a heavy crop of black, messy fruit, and the seeds, both fallen and distributed by birds, sprout profusely in gardens and must be pulled by hand. Count this as a weed tree. You can see it as a street tree on Almond Ave. or as a huge handsome specimen, growing in a lawn at 1035 Crooked Creek Dr.

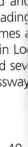

Liquidambar styraciflua
AMERICAN SWEET GUM

This beautiful, deciduous tree has maple-shaped leaves which turn brilliant shades of red and orange in the fall. It grows to 40-60 feet in height with branches from the ground up, spreading to 25 feet. Mature trees set a profuse crop of 1 inch, round, prickly burrs that are sometimes a nuisance. The roots are invasive and can crack pavement. Many liquidambars are planted in Los Altos. There are nine of these trees in a row at 1585 Ben Roe Drive at Newcastle Drive and several at 395 Los Altos Ave. at Yerba Santa. Many are planted in the meridian of Foothill Expressway.

Liquidambar orientalis
ORIENTAL SWEET GUM

⇩

Shorter than its American cousin, Liquidambar orientalis grows 20-30 feet tall and wide. It has deeply lobed, lacy leaves that turn yellow in late fall, a very short leafless period and smaller seed-balls. It is resistant to oak root fungus. There is an example at 400 E. Edith.

⇨

Liriodendron tulipifera
TULIP TREE

Tulip tree gets its name from its unique tulip-shaped leaves and flowers. This deciduous tree reaches 50-70 feet in height with a spread of 25-35 feet. Light green, three lobed leaves put on a show of yellow in the fall. Large greenish flowers with orange centers in the shape of tulips bloom in summertime but hide in the leaves. It is a good shade tree and resistant to oak root fungus, but it has shallow roots which make it difficult to garden under. Commonly planted in Los Altos, specimens can be seen at 1395 Montclair, 805 University, and in front of and in the parking lot at the Hillview Community Center.

41

Lyonothamnus floribundus asplenifolius
CATALINA IRONWOOD

This native California evergreen is an unpredictable tree that varies from slender to wide spreading and often assumes picturesque forms. It grows moderately fast to the height of 20-35 feet and a spread of 15 feet. The dark green leaves are either fern-like or blade-shaped and scalloped. The bark is reddish brown and peels in long strips which turn gray. During June and July tiny, white flowers appear in showy, large, flat clusters. It has a bad habit of sprouting from the base. It needs excellent drainage. See a specimen in the Hillview Community Center parking lot.

Magnolia (deciduous)
CHINESE TULIP TREE

There are many spectacular varieties of deciduous magnolia in Los Altos. Their handsome grey bark and shapely branching make them attractive even when leafless. Most bloom with massive displays of big flowers in late winter, but some can bloom in early January and are subject to frost damage. Varieties vary from 15-40 feet tall and up to 40 feet wide. Some worth a trip to see in bloom in late February/early March are at 1621 Holt Ave, 146 E. Portola Ave., and 66 N. Avalon. Another variety, **M. liliiflora**, the Lily Magnolia, blooms over a long time in late spring and summer. See it at 546 and 667 University.

42

Magnolia grandiflora
SOUTHERN MAGNOLIA

This beautiful, broad-leafed evergreen is a well-rounded, wide-spreading tree with large, glossy, dark-green leaves. The huge, fragrant flowers form pure white, cup-shaped blossoms. The tree blooms all year, profusely from April to July. Its shallow roots can lift pavement and there is messy drop of leaves and petals all summer. There are a number of varieties ranging from 20-80 feet tall and 15-60 feet wide. See it at the police station at 1 San Antonio Rd., at 612 Stardust Lane, 666 Milverton, 740 and 776 University Ave., and many other locations in Los Altos.

Photo by Susan Moss

Malus
CRABAPPLE

There are hundreds of varieties of flowering crabapple. They have flowers ranging from pale pink to red. Yellow or red fruits hang on the tree after the leaves have fallen. They are small trees and some have a weeping form. Be sure to plant a disease resistant type and one that does not require winter chilling. A deep pink variety, **'Robinson'** with bronzy leaves is on the Los Altos list of recommended street trees and on PG&E's list of trees to plant under power lines. A variety with pink buds opening to white flowers called Malus floribunda or 'Japanese Flowering Crabapple' is widely planted in Los Altos. See crabapples at 270 Alta Vista, 276 Angela, 915 Berry at Russell, 449 Cypress, 145 and 169 Marvin, and 1207 Thurston.

43

Maytenus boaria
MAYTEN TREE

This graceful tree from South America looks like a small weeping willow with long pendulous branchlets hanging down. It is evergreen with narrow 1-2 inch leaves. Although the foliage is dense, the tree has a delicate or lacy appearance. It grows slowly to 20, 30 or even 50 feet tall and wide. It needs good drainage and is resistant to oak root fungus. Deep irrigation is necessary to keep the tree from sending up shoots from the roots. Los Altos recommends this as a good street tree. Specimens can be found at 65 N. Avalon Dr., 778 Altos Oaks, 1396 Morton Ave, and 480 Torwood.

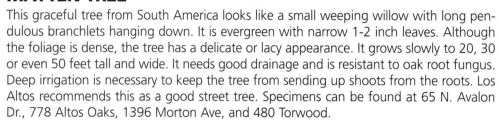

Melaleuca rhaphiophylla
SWAMP PAPERBARK

These evergreen natives of Australia are drought tolerant and grow 12-45 feet tall with a spread of 9-24 feet. Masses of showy, creamy white flowers bloom in late spring and summer. The papery brownish gray bark is very distinctive. The leaves are soft, needle-like, and about 1-2 inches long. The picture was taken at 176 E. Edith. You can also see M. rhaphiophylla at 70 Angela, 205 Coronado, and 110 W. Edith. **M. styphelioides** is recommended by Los Altos as a medium-size street or lawn tree. It has a somewhat weeping habit, white, bottlebrush-shaped flowers and small, prickly leaves.

44

Melia azedarach
CHINABERRY or HONEY TREE

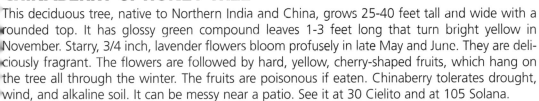

This deciduous tree, native to Northern India and China, grows 25-40 feet tall and wide with a rounded top. It has glossy green compound leaves 1-3 feet long that turn bright yellow in November. Starry, 3/4 inch, lavender flowers bloom profusely in late May and June. They are deliciously fragrant. The flowers are followed by hard, yellow, cherry-shaped fruits, which hang on the tree all through the winter. The fruits are poisonous if eaten. Chinaberry tolerates drought, wind, and alkaline soil. It can be messy near a patio. See it at 30 Cielito and at 105 Solana.

Metasequoia glypto-stroboides
DAWN REDWOOD

This is a very unusual tree, a holdover from prehistoric times, found in a few isolated sites in China in the 1940s. Although a distant relative of Coast Redwoods, it is deciduous. The soft light green needles turn bronzy in the fall. The trunk is red when young, but older trees have dark fissured bark, smoother than that of Coast Redwood. It is a good lawn tree, requiring regular water and good drainage, and it is resistant to oak root fungus. It grows very fast when young, reaching 90 feet or more. The photo was taken at 385 Monterey Place. There are also good examples at 710 Berry, and at 1413 Oak Drive.

45

Morus alba 'Fruitless'
FRUITLESS MULBERRY

⇩

This deciduous tree provides good shade in summer and yellow color in the fall. It is a good street tree, but is difficult to garden under because of greedy surface roots. It requires careful pruning when young to allow the trunk to develop strength to carry the long branches. Fruited forms are not recommended because the fruit is profuse and has inky juice that stains pavement and clothing. It grows 30-50 feet high and wide and likes regular water. Leaves are lobed and 6 inches long and wide. Specimens can be found on the side of the Youth Center in Civic Center, as a street tree on Los Altos Avenue, and at 130 and 580 Los Altos Avenue.

Myoporum laetum
MYOPORUM

This broad-leafed evergreen is a native of New Zealand. It grows exceptionally fast to 30 feet tall and 20 feet wide and forms a very round silhouette. The narrow, 3-4 inch leaves are dark and shiny. The small white flowers are pretty close up, but don't show at a distance. Tiny purple fruit follows them. This tree is subject to frost damage below 24° F. See one next to the multipurpose room at Hillview Community Center and two at 251 Covington.

Nyssa sylvatica
TUPELO TREE

This deciduous tree is noted for beautiful fall colors, yellow and orange turning to red. It leafs out late, but has handsome crooked branches and dark, mahogany colored bark. It likes moist, well-drained acid soil, but will tolerate some drought. It is very deep rooted. It grows at a slow to moderate pace to 30-50 feet tall and 15-25 feet wide. Specimens can be seen at 530 Shelby, and at Pilgrim Haven on Pine Lane one building to the left of the main entrance.

Olea europaea
OLIVE

This is an ancient beauty with gray-green leaves and gnarled trunk. The long-lived ever-green trees take well to pruning and fit into gardens happily. Olive trees adapt to a variety of soils, climate, and watering regimes. They grow about 30 feet high and 30 feet wide. The fruit is inedible until it has been processed. Fruit drop can be messy and reseed-ing is a problem. You can spray with special hormones to control fruiting. A fruitless variety with little pollen called 'Swan Hill' is planted in the San Antonio median directly across from City Hall. Big fruit-bearing olive trees can be seen at the corner of Raquel and Hacienda, at 480 Harrington, at City Hall, and in the Foothill Expressway median between Main and Edith.

47

Parrotia persica
PERSIAN PARROTIA

This tree is interesting in all seasons. In late winter or early spring it is covered with tiny flowers with red stamens and wooly brown bracts. New leaves (3-6 inch scalloped ovals) are reddish purple, becoming dark green through the summer. Then, in the fall, the best show starts with the leaves turning yellow, then pink, and then bright red and rusty, often with all colors on a leaf at the same time. Parrotia grows 15-35 feet high and wide. A good lawn tree, it requires a moderate amount of water. See it at 968 Crooked Creek Drive.

Paulownia tomentosa
EMPRESS or SOUTHERN
DRAGON TREE

This deciduous tree grows very quickly to 40-50 feet tall with equal spread. It makes a spectacular show of fragrant, lilac-blue, trumpet-shaped flowers in clusters in May. The olive-shaped flower buds are brown and form in fall and winter, looking like old seedpods. Two-inch seedpods form after the flowers and hang on through the winter, mixed in with bud clusters. The large, light green leaves give this tree a tropical look. It likes regular water and is difficult to garden under. There is one growing at 610 Campbell.

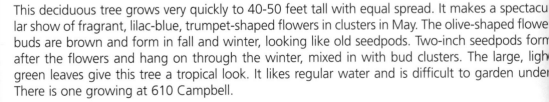

Persea americana
AVOCADO

This is a handsome evergreen tree with large, broad, glossy, dark yellow-green leaves. It is frost sensitive and requires warmer temperatures than found in Los Altos in order to fruit well. It needs excellent drainage. It grows 20-40 feet high with a wider spread. There are nice specimens at 610 Jay St., and 1241 and 1265 Thurston.

Phoenix canariensis
CANARY ISLAND PALM

This massive and wide-spreading palm is quite commonly planted in Los Altos, often associated with the older, historic houses. It has long, arching, feather-like leaves that droop heavily near the bottom of the dense crown. It grows from 10-50 feet high and wide. Enormous clusters of small yellow flowers hang down and are followed by small dates. It likes regular water. Historic records say that Spanish missionaries brought seeds of this palm from the Canary Islands in the mid-1700s and planted them at the California Missions. A few examples are at 645 Distel Dr., History House at Hillview Community Center, 684 Jay St., and the Northwest corner of San Antonio and Edith.

Picea engelmannii
ENGELMANN SPRUCE

This great evergreen with blue-green needles is native to Northern California and the Pacific Northwest. Pyramidal in shape and densely branched to the ground, it can grow to 150 feet in height. The needles are softer than those of Colorado Blue Spruce. It requires little water. See it in Singer Plaza, corner of Main and State St. and at 671 Covington.

Picea pungens
COLORADO BLUE SPRUCE

This beautiful blue-green to gray-blue evergreen with sharp needles has a sturdy, upright, pyramidal form with branches that stay on down to the ground. It can grow to 80-100 feet with a spread of 40-50 feet but there are named varieties that grow smaller and are a better choice for gardens. It prefers dry soil. There are nice specimens at 623 Almond, 675 Berry, 175 Galli, 461 Hacienda, 128 Sheridan and 1218 Thurston.

Pinus canariensis
CANARY ISLAND PINE

This graceful pine is distinguishable by its long, pendant, gray-green needles in clusters of three, 9-12 inches long, which droop from slender spreading branches. The cones are 4-9 inches long and glossy brown. It grows rapidly to 60-80 feet and 20-35 feet wide. This tree has fissured reddish bark and presents a delicate appearance unusual in pines. It is resistant to oak root fungus, is drought tolerant, and has roots that do not destroy pavement. It is recommended by Los Altos as a large evergreen street tree. See it at 101 and 112 Garland Way, 1165 Miguel, 760 Orange, and 450 Pine Lane.

Pinus eldarica
ELDARICA PINE

Tall, pyramidal, and fast growing, this pine grows to 40 feet in 15 years. The needles are in pairs, dark green and 5-6 inches long. The cones, which hang on the tree for several years, are 3 inches long, oval to oblong and reddish brown. Los Altos recommends it as an excellent Monterey Pine substitute, disease resistant and tolerant of many soils. See it at 14 N. Avalon Drive and the NW corner of El Monte and Foothill Expressway.

51

Pinus mugo mugo
MUGHO PINE

Mugho pine is a shrubby, round little pine that seldom grows to more than 4 feet. The 2 inch long dark green needles are in pairs and densely packed along the branches. It is excellent for small gardens. See it a 486 Santa Barbara and at 801 University.

Pinus pinea
ITALIAN STONE PINE

A heavy, flat umbrella-like top distinguishes this variety, although in youth it is round and bushy. The needles, in pairs, are bright green and densely packed along the branches. It grows moderately fast to 40-80 feet tall and wide. The cones have edible seeds (pine nuts). It makes a dramatic statement in the garden. See specimens at 11 Angela, 110 N. Gordon, and 460 Tyndall.

52

Pinus radiata
MONTEREY PINE

⇩

This native of the California coast is shallow rooted and subject to many pests and diseases. It is widely planted in Los Altos. If you have one, give it deep water to encourage deeper roots. It grows rapidly (6 feet a year) and will reach 50 feet in 12 years. The needles are bright green, in clusters of three, 3-7 inches long. The cones are lopsided, in clusters, and hang onto the tree persistently. Examples are at 145 El Monte, 265 Mt. Hamilton, 1540 Oak, 220 Yerba Santa, and next to the Youth Center in Civic Center.

Pinus thunbergii
JAPANESE BLACK PINE

⇧

This handsome pine is distinguished by white new growth that looks like candles. It takes well to pruning, so it is often grown as a bonsai or a pyramidal Christmas tree. It might be 40 feet tall or 4 feet tall depending on how it is pruned. The needles are bright green, stiff, and 3-4 inches long. The granite Los Altos markers at the town entrances contain Japanese Black Pine. See it at town entrances at El Monte and Springer, San Antonio and El Camino, Foothill Expressway and Main, and at 521 Guadalupe Dr.

Pistacia chinensis
CHINESE PISTACHE

This is the Los Altos signature tree that turns the town brilliant red in the fall. In the downtown triangle the trees are lit with tiny white lights in the Holiday season. The deciduous tree is round headed with arching branches that spread widely from a short, stout trunk. The 8-10 inch long leaves are composed of 10-16 narrow, 2-4 inch leaflets. Female trees bear heavy bunches of red to black fruit that attract birds. It grows slowly to 30-60 feet tall and wide. Very adaptable, it can take lawn water or drought and many types of soil. It is resistant to oak root fungus but subject to verticillium wilt. It is pest free and has a non-destructive root system. See it in many places, but especially in the Downtown triangle and next to City Council chambers at City Hall.

Pittosporum undulatum
VICTORIAN BOX

This graceful, tall shrub or small tree has glossy green, wavy-margined leaves that densely cover the round crown. The tree also bears intensely fragrant, white flowers in spring. It has a beautiful branching pattern that can be made visible by judicious pruning. It grows at a moderate rate to 15 by 15 feet and then more slowly to 30 feet. The roots are strong and can become invasive with age. Sticky orange fallen fruit can be a problem. Los Altos recommends it as a street tree. See it at 47 S. Gordon, 640 Orange, 11 View St., and in the meridian of San Antonio between Alma and Almond.

Platanus racemosa
CALIFORNIA SYCAMORE

There are two kinds of platanus planted in Los Altos. Both have creamy tan colored bark that sheds in patches and brown ball-shaped seed clusters. Big, light green, rough surfaced leaves, shaped like maple leaves with 3 to 5 lobes, have white wooly undersides. The trees are deciduous. Both are subject to mildew, but there are some mildew resistant varieties. They grow fast to 30-80 feet tall and 20-50 feet wide. Platanus racemosa, California Sycamore, is a big California native that prefers to grow along stream banks. See specimens at 1551 Ben Roe, Shoup Park on University Ave., and at McKenzie Park on Fremont Ave.

Platanus x acerifolia
LONDON PLANE TREE

London Plane Tree looks very similar to California Sycamore and has the same characteristics. The leaves may be somewhat smaller. This tree is often pruned back to knobby branch stubs to keep its size within limits. Left alone it will grow to 30-80 feet tall and 20-50 feet wide. It is recommended by the City of Los Altos as a street tree. See it on Almond Ave. in front of Los Altos High School, at 11 Sylvian Way, and at 751 University.

Podocarpus gracilor
FERN PINE

This graceful tree grows to 20-60 feet tall and 10-20 feet wide. It has glossy light green to dark green leaves 2-4 inches long. Podocarpus is one of the cleanest, most pest free trees for street, lawn or patio. Examples are at 322 Almond Ave., 182 Eleanor Ave., 1575 Oak Ave., and at Shoup Park near the creek placard. There is a **Podocarpus macrophyllus**, Yew Pine, which is more narrow and tall, with bigger leaves, at 271 State Street on the parking plaza.

Prunus amygdalus (or dulcis)
ALMOND

These deciduous trees produce delicious nuts and grow 25-30 feet tall and wide. They have showy pale pink flowers in early February and gray-green leaves 5 inches long. Some require cross-pollination with a second variety, so, if you plant only one tree, plant one grafted with several varieties. They need deep soil and good drainage. There were almond orchards at one time in Los Altos. The pictured specimen is at the corner of E. Edith and Eleanor Ave. See it also at 157 Arbuelo Way.

Prunus armeniaca
APRICOT

Los Altos at one time had large apricot orchards. The remnants of one surround City Hall and the Youth Center. Many homes have one or two of these trees left over from the old orchards. Apricots put on a good show of white or pink flowers in early spring. They are deciduous and grow 15-20 feet tall and wide. The delicious fruit should be thinned early to encourage larger fruit. The trees should be pruned in late summertime. They are subject to some diseases and may require dormant spray before and after flowering. Do not leave old fruit on the tree or on the ground. The trees pictured are at City Hall.

Prunus species
FRUITING PLUM

Most have showy double white flowers in late February. They have bright green, shiny, ovate leaves. Fruits vary from small to large and almost any color of the rainbow. Pruning encourages fruit production and keeps the fruit low enough to pick easily. The picture was taken at 264 W. Portola. Another is at 65 N. Avalon Dr.

Prunus cerasifera
FLOWERING PLUM

Flowering plums are deciduous and grow 15-35 feet tall and 12-20 feet wide. Los Altos recommends them as small street trees and PG&E recommends them for planting under power lines. The most commonly planted flowering plums in Los Altos are varieties called Thundercloud (light pink single flowers, purple foliage all summer, nice edible fruits in some years), Krauters Vesuvius (no fruit, flowers light pink, almost black foliage), Hollywood (tallest variety, sets good 2 inch fruit, has pale pink single flowers and leaves that are green on top and red underneath), and Blireiana (bright pink double flowers, purple foliage turning to bronzy green in the summer, few fruits). P. blireiana has problems with aphids in the spring. See examples of flowering plums at 50 Cielito, 1586 Morton, 740 University, 150 W. Edith, and on Stonehaven at Montclaire Park.

Prunus serrulata
JAPANESE FLOWERING CHERRY

There are many varieties of flowering cherry. All are deciduous, require good drainage and are good to garden under. They bloom anywhere from early to late spring and have flowers that range from dark pink to white and single to double. Some blossom before the leaves appear, others have flowers among the leaves. Some are weeping; some have orange-red leaves in the fall. They grow to 30 feet high and as wide. PG&E recommends flowering cherries for planting under power lines. The Furuichi family, who own the Los Altos Nursery, brought variety 'Ben Hoshi' to the United States in 1958. The original tree is at the nursery on Hawthorne Ave. The cherries pictured are on the San Antonio side of the library. Others are at 453 Cypress Dr., 182 Cherry, 891 Stagi, 182 Eleanor, and 318 Yerba Buena. The variety **'Kwanzan'**, vase shaped, with double pink flowers, is recommended as a street tree in Los Altos. See examples at 782 Covington, at 746 University, and on Los Altos Ave. near Stratford Lane.

Pseudotsuga macrocarpa
BIGCONE SPRUCE

This tree is not a spruce but rather an evergreen relative of Douglas Fir. It has cones 4-7 inches long and 2-3 inches wide, distinctively larger than those of Douglas Fir. The cones hang down and make quite a show. It is native to Southern California and grows to 60 feet tall and 30 feet wide. It is not fussy about soil and takes drought or regular water. See it at 954 Golden Way and at 580 Orange Ave.

Pseudotsuga menziesii
DOUGLAS FIR

This evergreen is native to mountains from Washington to Monterey. It grows to 80-160 feet tall and 20-30 feet wide, dropping lower branches as it grows older. It is common in Los Altos and can be gardened under. Its oblong, pendant cones are 3 inches long with 3 prongs on each bract. They grow in all soils and can take drought or regular water. Some examples are at 141 Alvarado, 141 S. Gordon, 1253 Thurston, 517 Tyndall, and at the First Church of Christ Scientist Los Altos at 401 University.

Pyrus calleryana
DECIDUOUS FLOWERING PEAR

These trees have a brilliant display of white flowers in March. Glossy dark green leaves in summer and fall turn copper and purplish red in early winter. They are not fussy about soil, but may be subject to fireblight. They are recommended as street trees by Los Altos. Three varieties are common in Los Altos. 'Bradford' grows to 50 feet tall and 30 feet wide. See it at 236 Galli. 'Aristocrat' is pyramidal in form to 40 feet tall and 20 feet wide. See it at the Los Altos United Methodist Church parking lot at Magdalena and Foothill Expressway. 'Chanticleer' is columnar to 40 feet tall and 20 feet wide. It has the best branching structure. See it at History House and Bus Barn Theater.

Pyrus kawakamii
EVERGREEN PEAR

This broadleaved evergreen is renowned for pendulous branches, glossy leaves, and clusters of white flowers in January and February. The leaves sometimes turn yellow and red just before the flowers bloom. It is somewhat messy, dropping leaves and small dry fruits. It grows to 15-30 feet tall with an equal spread. It is widely planted in Los Altos. See it at 752 and 894 University and on the corner of Yerba Santa and Los Altos Ave.

Quercus agrifolia
COAST LIVE OAK or ENCINA

These evergreen native oaks are very long lived. They grow to 40-70 feet tall with a 70 foot spread. They have glossy, convex, spiny 1-2 inch leaves, the older of which tend to drop all at once in early spring. The smooth gray limbs and branches twist in picturesque ways. Young trees grow fast with water; older trees prefer no water in summer. Never add soil above the established root-line. Doing so can kill the tree. Coast Live Oak is recommended by Los Altos as a street tree for large areas. A few of the beautiful, historic old oaks in Los Altos are at 58 Alma Ct., 215 Coronado, Hillview Community Center, History House, 600 and 671 Milverton, 1166 Miramonte, Mckenzie Park, 1065 Muir Way, in the center island on Rinconada, at Shoup Park, 234 Live Oak Lane, and 749 University.

Quercus douglasii
BLUE OAK

This beautiful California native is deciduous and has shallowly lobed, definitely blue-green leaves which turn pink or orange in the fall. The bark is light grey and somewhat checkered. It grows 30-50 feet tall and 40-70 feet wide. The acorns are ovate with a sharply pointed tip and flat cap. See specimens at 898 and 950 University.

61

Quercus ilex
HOLLY OAK

This evergreen oak is native to the Mediterranean region. Smaller than most oaks, it grows 30-50 feet tall and wide. The leaves are narrow ovals 1-3 inches long. They are dark green on top and hairy gray or yellowish underneath. The cap covers nearly half of the 1 inch long acorns which fall in October. Specimens are at 55 Arbuelo Way and 600 Guadalupe Dr.

Quercus lobata
VALLEY OAK

This magnificent, long-lived California native oak grows bigger than Coast Live Oak, more than 70 feet with a wider spread. It is deciduous and has deeply cut, round-lobed leaves 2-4 inches long. See leaf shape on Table of Contents page. Older trees have very picturesque twisted branches and checkered dark gray bark. It can be messy to live with because of a constant rain of debris. Acorns are about 1 inch long, covered about 1/3 of the length by a bumpy cap. Valley Oak is somewhat resistant to oak root fungus. Specimens can be seen at City Hall, 1440 Braddale, Golden Way at Lincoln, 677 Linden, the Los Altos United Methodist Church and Rancho Shopping Center on Magdalena/Miramonte and Foothill Expressway, and in Lincoln Park on University.

Quercus rubra
RED OAK

This deciduous oak is native to eastern U.S. It grows to 60-70 feet tall and 50 feet wide. The leaves are 5-8 inches long and 4-6 inches wide with several sharp-pointed lobes. They are red-orange when young, turn bronze-green in the summer and orange again in the fall. Brown leaves hang on the tree all winter. Roundish, 3/4 inch acorns with points and shallow caps take two years to mature. Deep roots make it easy to garden under. See it at 37 N. Avalon Dr. and 2080 Robinhood Lane.

Quercus suber
CORK OAK

This is an evergreen oak with distinctive thick bark that is used for making corks. The 3 inch oval leaves are shiny dark green above and gray underneath. It is a good garden tree. It grows slowly to 30-60 feet high with equal spread. It is very drought tolerant and needs little fertilizer. Los Altos recommends it as a street tree. Nice specimens can be seen at 451 Cherry, 1097 Muir Way, 381 Raquel, and in Shoup Park near the tot playground.

Rhus lancea
AFRICAN SUMAC ⇩

This slow growing graceful evergreen tree has shiny dark green leaves composed of three 4-5 inch long leaflets that hang down like a willow tree. It is drought tolerant and grows slowly to 20-30 feet high and 20-35 feet wide. See it at 448 Rinconada and 890 University.

⇧ ## Robinia pseudoacacia 'Frisia'
GOLDEN SUNBURST LOCUST

This deciduous tree comes from eastern United States. Young leaves are orange and then turn yellow as they mature. It grows quickly to 50 feet high and 25 feet wide. It tolerates drought and poor soil. Suckers can be a problem. The leaves are divided into as many as 20 oval leaflets. Seeds, leaves, and bark are poisonous if eaten. See it at 430 Guadalupe (on the Raquel side), 1231 Thurston and 200 University.

Robinia x ambigua 'Decaisneana'
PINK LOCUST

Pink Locust is covered with clusters of sweet-pea shaped flowers in April and May. It is deciduous and grows 40-50 feet tall and 20 feet wide. Leaf shape is similar to Idaho Locust but Pink Locust is taller and narrower. All other comments are the same for all three Robinia trees. Leaves, seeds, and bark are poisonous if eaten. See this one at 451 Rinconada and 24 Marvin.

Robinia x ambigua 'Idahoensis'
IDAHO LOCUST

Idaho Locust has beautiful clusters of red-violet flowers from mid-spring to early summer. The leaves are light green and divided into many oval leaflets. It is deciduous and grows fairly fast to 40 feet tall and 30 feet wide. It tolerates drought and does not reseed, but it has aggressive roots. Leaves, seeds, and bark are poisonous if eaten. Los Altos recommends it as a street tree. See it at 527 Orange, on the corner of Orange and Sheridan, and at the Community Center on Hillview.

Salix babylonica
WEEPING WILLOW

These beautiful trees need a great deal of water and are weak wooded and short lived. They have shallow, invasive roots. The 3-6 inch long medium-green leaves appear early and hang on late. They grow to 40 feet tall and wider. The one pictured is at 1840 Granger. There is also one at 24511 Summerhill.

Sapium sebiferum
CHINESE TALLOW TREE

This deciduous tree leafs out late, but is very interesting the rest of the year. The 2-3 inch, heart-shaped, light green leaves flutter in any little breeze. In late summer, long catkins appear with much pollen, followed by clusters of grayish, waxy fruits. In late fall the leaves turn red, purple and orange. It grows to 30 feet tall by 20 feet wide. Do not plant it near a creek because it self-seeds and can become a pest in wet environments. Tallow Tree is recommended as a street tree by Los Altos. It is resistant to oak root fungus. There are specimens at 1 Cypress Ct., 234 E. Edith, the Los Altos Lutheran Church on Cuesta and El Monte, and the Los Altos United Methodist Church at 655 Magdalena (corner of Foothill Expressway).

Schinus molle
CALIFORNIA PEPPER TREE

This beautiful, drought-tolerant evergreen tree is native to the Peruvian Andes. It has gracefully weeping, long leaves composed of many leaflets. Old trees have picturesque, gnarly trunks. Clusters of pink berries decorate the tree in the fall and winter. It grows quickly to 25-40 feet high and wide and requires little care. However, it has many drawbacks such as constant litter and greedy surface roots and is susceptible to oak root fungus. Los Altos recommends it as medium size street tree. See it as a street tree on Covington between El Monte and Springer. This photo is taken at 167 E. Edith. There are also some on University north of Main St.

Sequoia
sempervirens
COAST REDWOOD

This beautiful California native evergreen has soft, dark green or blue green needles in flat feathery sprays and small (1 inch) reddish brown cones. The bark is dark red-brown to grayish and deeply furrowed. This tree grows rapidly to 100 (or even 350) feet tall and is the tallest tree in the world. It likes regular water and does well in gardens, though it will dominate the space quickly. There are many planted in Los Altos and the city recommends it as a large street tree. Some along San Antonio Road have succumbed to disease. Noteworthy redwoods are at the intersection of Springer and El Monte and in the city park called Redwood Grove on University. In addition, there is a slow growing cultivar at 628 Cuesta.

67

Sequoiadendron giganteum
GIANT SEQUOIA

This is the Giant Sequoia that grows in Yosemite and other Sierra Nevada locations where 3000 year old trees reach enormous proportions. Young trees, however, do well in large gardens reaching 60-100 feet high and 30-50 feet wide. They grow slower than Coast Redwoods and need less water. The leaves are prickly, composed of overlapping gray-green scales. The 2-3 inch cones are reddish brown. Branches stay on clear to the ground, so leave a lot of room for this tree. See it at 660 Templebar Way, 1082 St. Joseph Ave., and 785 Altos Oaks Dr.

Syragus romanzoffianum
QUEEN PALM

This graceful Palm tree has a dense head of feathery, blue-green fronds, 8-15 feet long, which arch out gracefully from the trunk. It grows quickly to 15-40 feet high and 10-25 feet wide. It makes an excellent patio, street, or tubbed specimen. The tree is very hardy, presenting no maintenance problems other than its need for a deep watering once a month. See it at 1000 Rilma Lane.

Tamarix
TAMARISK

⇩

Like a pink cloud in spring, Tamarisk is covered with tiny pink flowers that later turn brown. The leaves are also tiny. Tamarisk grows to about 25 feet high and wide. It requires little water and full sun. It grows readily from 1/2 inch cuttings placed in the ground and watered until roots form. It can become invasive. Do not plant it near streams. See it peeking over the fence at the fire station on Almond.

⇨

Tilia cordata
LINDEN

This deciduous tree is a native of Europe. Leaves are heart-shaped, dark green above and silvery underneath. Small clusters of very fragrant, creamy flowers in July turn into little seedpods each surrounded by a two-lobed, pale green or white, papery bract, 2 inches long, giving the tree the look of being covered with white butterflies all summer long. It grows densely to 30-50 feet high and 15-30 feet wide. It needs regular water, but is adaptable to all kinds of growing conditions. Aphids can be a problem for patio trees. See it at 246 Eleanor, 184 Hawthorne and 863 University. At 863 University there is also a **Tilia platyphyllos**, Large Leaf Linden, with 3 by 6 inch leaves and unlobed bracts about 6 inch long and 1 inch wide. It blooms in late June.

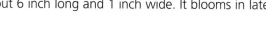

Tristaniaopsis laurina 'Elegans'
BRISBANE BOX

This evergreen Australian native has smooth, mahogany colored bark that sloughs off to reveal white new bark underneath. It is slow growing, eventually reaching 10-45 feet high and 5-30 feet wide. It needs regular water. Narrow, 4 inch long leaves and clusters of fragrant, small yellow flowers in late spring distinguish it from **Lophostemon confertus**, which it resembles. Lophostemon, which used to be called Tristania conferta, has similar bark, but 6 inch leaves and white, 3/4 inch flowers in the summertime. It is a good street or lawn tree and requires little water. See Lophostemon at 164 Doud and 168 Alvarado. See Tristaniopsis at 555 Stardust Lane, 795 A Altos Oaks Dr., 752 University, and the SW corner of the shopping center at El Camino and San Antonio, near Loucks.

Ulmus parvifolia
CHINESE OR EVERGREEN ELM

This graceful elm is partially evergreen in Los Altos, dropping about half its leaves in winter. The pale tan bark sheds in patches to show orange new bark underneath. The tree is spreading, almost weeping in structure. Leaves are leathery, dark green, 1-2 1/2 inches long on long branchlets. It makes a good patio, shade, or street tree with careful pruning, growing fast to 40-60 feet high and 50-70 feet wide. There are lots of these trees in Los Altos. A few nice examples are at 465 Gabilan, 545 Covington, 636 Palm, 243 Solana, and 660 and 803 University.

Umbellularia californica
CALIFORNIA BAY LAUREL

This California native grows very slowly to 75 feet high and 100 feet wide (but in gardens stays smaller). It has lance-shaped, 2-5 inch long, medium green leaves (shiny above and dull underneath) that smell wonderful when crushed and are used in cooking soups and stews. California Bay leaves are stronger than Grecian Laurel leaves so use smaller amounts in cooking. California Bay Laurel likes regular water but will tolerate drought. It has clusters of tiny yellow flowers in spring. Young trees can be seen at 124 and 204 Alvarado and 980 Covington.

Washingtonia robusta
MEXICAN FAN PALM

These tall stately palms are seen all over the area. Many older homes have them. They grow to 100 feet high and 10 feet wide. The fronds are fan-shaped, 3-6 feet long. A thatched residue of old leaves covers the bark near the top and should be removed periodically to prevent roof rats from living there. These palms get by on very little water. A few examples are at 1505 Grant Road, 834 Starlite Lane, and 2081 Stonehaven.

Xylosma congestum
XYLOSMA

Xylosma, often planted as a shrub, makes a charming multi-trunk tree, 12 feet high and wide with drooping side branches. New growth is bronze, while older leaves are shiny and yellowish green. It requires moderate water. Good examples are at Los Altos High School on Almond Ave., 887 Altos Oaks Dr., 390 Chamisal, and 617 Stardust Lane.

Zelkova serrata
JAPANESE ZELKOVA

This is a very good street or lawn tree, growing 50-90 feet high and wide, fairly drought tolerant and resistant to oak root fungus. It is well rounded with a short heavy trunk that divides into several stems. Its dark green leaves are 2-3 inches long with a saw-tooth edge. The foliage is dense and provides heavy shade. Zelkova is deciduous, and in the fall the leaves turn yellow, orange or dark red. The three colors in the photo are all Zelkovas. If you want a particular fall color, choose the tree in the fall. Kingswood Way and Thames Lane have Zelkovas as street trees. You can also see specimens at 149 Garland Way and 176 Osage.

72

LOS ALTOS RESIDENTIAL DESIGN GUIDELINES AND STREET TREE PLANTING LIST

Residential design guidelines for Los Altos recommend planting trees in the front yard to soften the impact of development and for screening along rear and side property lines. They encourage planting street trees in the city right-of-way, if possible. (This requires an encroachment permit to make sure underground utilities and parking needs are not impacted.) Property owners (except in commercial zoning districts) are responsible for maintenance of trees on their property, including those adjacent to their property in the city right-of-way (see Municipal Code Section 9.20.025), providing 9 feet of vertical clearance for pedestrians and 13 feet of clearance for vehicles. Property owners who have any questions about care or planting of street trees should contact the Los Altos Community Development Department.

City of Los Altos Street Tree Planting List

Category I: Trees that grow over 40 feet and need minimum 6 foot wide planting areas: Do not plant under utility wires.

Deciduous Species:

Celtis australis	EUROPEAN HACKBERRY
Celtis sinensis	CHINESE HACKBERRY
Ginko biloba 'Fairmount'	GINGKO
Liquidambar styraciflua 'Palo Alto'	SWEET GUM
Platanus acerifolia	LONDON PLANE TREE
Quercus lobata	VALLEY OAK

Evergreen species:

Cinnamomum camphora	CAMPHOR TREE
Cedrus deodora	DEODAR CEDAR
Pinus canariensis	CANARY ISLAND PINE
Pinus eldarica	ELDARICA PINE
Sequoia sempervirens	COAST REDWOOD
Quercus agrifolia	COAST LIVE OAK

Category II: Trees that grow to 40 feet and require less than 6 feet of growing space:

Deciduous Species

Fraxinus augustifolia 'Raywood'	RAYWOOD ASH
Koelreuteria bipinnata	CHINESE FLAME TREE
Koelreuteria paniculata	GOLDENRAIN TREE
Melaleuca styphelioides	PRICKLY MELALEUCA
Pistacia chinensis	CHINESE PISTACHE
Pyrus calleryana cultivars	FLOWERING PEAR
Robinia ambigua 'Idahoensis'	IDAHO LOCUST

Evergreen species:

Ceratonia siliqua	CAROB TREE
Geijera parviflora	AUSTRALIAN WILLOW
Maytenus boaria	MAYTEN TREE
Pittosporum undulatum	VICTORIAN BOX
Quercus suber	CORK OAK
Schinus molle	CALIFORNIA PEPPER TREE

Category III: Trees that grow no higher than 30 feet:

Deciduous species:

Cercis canadensis	EASTERN REDBUD
Lagerstroemia indica	CRAPE MYRTLE
Malus 'Robinson'	ROBINSON CRABAPPLE
Prunus cerasifera cultivars	PURPLE LEAF PLUM
Prunus serrulata 'Kwanzan'	FLOWERING CHERRY
Sapium sebiferum	CHINESE TALLOW TREE

CITY OF LOS ALTOS TREE PROTECTION REGULATIONS

In 1993 the Los Altos City Council recognized the economic and aesthetic values of the diversity of trees in the city. The Council stated "Trees help stabilize the soil, enhance views, provide privacy, counteract pollutants, maintain the climatic balance, decrease wind velocities, provide shelter for and feed birds and other wildlife and provide shelter for and feed birds and other wildlife and provide fragrance and color." Trees are very important to the character of the city and add value to individual properties.

Tree protection regulations are set out in Title 11, chapter 11.08 of the Los Altos Municipal Code and Resolution 93-8, which states, "The development and redevelopment of the City often necessitates the removal of trees, thereby contributing to their depletion; and it is necessary to protect and manage these valuable assets and their habitat to protect the health, safety and welfare of the citizens of Los Altos." To avoid long-term problems, those involved in the planning process, such as property owner, contractor, engineer or architect and arborist should be aware of the ordinances applying to trees.

At time of publication, the tree protection regulations and resolution automatically protect the following trees if they measure 48" in circumference 48" above natural grade.
1. Quercus, e.g. Live Oak, Valley Oak, Cork Oak, etc.
2. Sequoia, e.g. Coast Redwood
3. Platanus, e.g. London Plane Tree, California Sycamore
4. Umbellularia, e.g. Bay Laurel

They also require a permit for removal of any of the following: trees designated as "protected" by City Council resolution, trees designated as "heritage" by the Historical Commission, trees required to be retained in a development review application, trees located on property zoned other than R1, trees located on undeveloped property or on developed property where additional development is expected to occur.

The "heritage" designation is based on the finding that the tree has character, interest or value as part of the cultural, educational, economic, agricultural, social, indigenous or historical heritage of the city. It is important that arborists, developers and homeowners be aware of these restrictions. Property owners or neighboring property owners may ask to have a tree protected in conjunction with a development review application. There are provisions in the ordinance for appeals and emergency waivers.

The regulations also include criteria for determination of the permit, regulations for tree removal and regulations for protection of trees during construction.

Damaging or removing protected trees without a permit is a misdemeanor subject to fines or replacement with trees of equal value.

The latest version of the Tree Protection Regulations is available on request at City Hall, or can be found online at:
http://ordlink.com/codes/losaltos/index.htm

TREES SUITABLE FOR UNDER POWER LINES

Trees under power lines are subject to being pruned by PG&E in an unnatural V or L shape to avoid damage to the lines. In order to avoid the need for pruning, PG&E recommends the following short trees for planting under power lines. They grow to about 20 ft. tall.

Deciduous Varieties:

Cercis canadensis	EASTERN REDBUD
Craetagus phaenopyrum	WASHINGTON THORN
Lagerstroemia indica	CRAPE MYRTLE
Malus 'Robinsonia'	CRABAPPLE
Prunus cerasifera	PURPLE LEAF PLUM
Pyrus calleryana	FLOWERING PEAR

Evergreen Varieties:

Arbutus unedo	STRAWBERRY TREE
Callistemon citrinus	BOTTLE BRUSH
Citrus	ORANGE, LEMON, etc.
Dodonaea	HOP BUSH
Eriobotrya deflexa	BRONZE LEAF LOQUAT
Geijera parveflora	AUSTRALIAN WILLOW
Heteromeles arbutifolia	TOYON
Oleander	OLEANDER
Pittosporum	PITTISPORUM
Pyrus kawakamii	EVERGREEN PEAR
Rhus lancea	AFRICAN SUMAC

TREES TO PLANT NEAR STREAMS

In "Guidelines for Stream Care," the Santa Clara Valley Water District (SCVWD) states that goals of stream care include
- Minimize erosion from property adjacent to streams
- Eliminate contamination from entering the streams
- Preserve the stream and the riparian zone in as natural a state as possible
- Restore native streamside vegetation where possible.

A healthy stream bank needs undisturbed soil and vegetation. Before doing any planting in or near the streamside area, first contact Santa Clara Valley Water District for applicable regulations and to obtain a free permit.

California natives that like to grow along your stretch of the creek are best. Consult with a native plant specialist or the California Native Plant Society. Members of the California Native Plant Society recently walked Adobe Creek in Los Altos and identified the following growing there now: Big Leaf Maple, Live Oak, Valley Oak, Blue Oak, California Buckeye, Black Walnut, California Sycamore, California Bay, Arroyo Willow, Scouler's Willow, and Blue Elderberry. Trees grown from seed collected in your reach of the stream are likely to be the healthiest. In addition, by directly seeding acorns and buckeye seed from local parent trees, your new trees will achieve independence from irrigation much sooner, or may need no irrigation at all.

Never use fertilizer or pesticides in a riparian zone and don't dump yard wastes into the creek corridor.

Some trees should never be planted near streams. They are invasive and do not provide the correct environment for the creek ecosystem. These include Acacia, Ailanthus, Almond, Evergreen Ash, Bamboo, Black Locust, Elm, Eucalyptus, Fig, Flowering Plum, Holly Oak, Ligustrum, London Plane Tree, Monterey Pine, Myoporum, Olive, Privet, Pepper trees, Tamarisk, and Walnut.

TREES RESISTANT TO OAK ROOT FUNGUS

Deciduous Varieties:

Acer macrophyllum	BIG LEAF MAPLE
Acer palmatum	JAPANESE MAPLE
Brachychiton populneus	BOTTLE TREE
Celtis australis and occidentalis	HACKBERRY
Cercis occidentalis	WESTERN REDBUD
Diospyros kaki	PERSIMMON
Erythrina crista-galli	CORAL TREE
Ficus carica	FIG
Fraxinus augustifolia 'Raywood'	RAYWOOD ASH
Ginkgo biloba	MAIDENHAIR TREE
Gleditsia triacanthos	HONEY LOCUST
Jacaranda mimosifolia	JACARANDA
Juglans californica	CALIFORNIA BLACK WALNUT
Liquidambar	SWEET GUM
Liriodendron tulipifera	TULIP TREE
Magnolia (deciduous)	CHINESE TULIP TREE
Malus	CRABAPPLE
Metasequoia glyptostroboides	DAWN REDWOOD
Morus alba 'fruitless'	FRUITLESS MULBERRY
Pistacia chinensis	CHINESE PISTACHE
Platanus	PLANE TREE, SYCAMORE
Pyrus calleryana	DECIDUOUS FLOWERING PEAR
Quercus lobata	VALLEY OAK
Sapium sebiferum	CHINESE TALLOW TREE
Zelkova serrata	JAPANESE ZELKOVA

Evergreen Varieties:

Arbutus menziesii	MADRONE
Persea americana	AVOCADO
Calocedrus decurrens	INCENSE CEDAR
Ceratonia siliqua	CAROB
Fraxinus uhdei	EVERGREEN ASH
Geijera parvifolia	AUSTRALIAN WILLOW
Ilex aquifolium	ENGLISH HOLLY
Maytenus boaria	MAYTEN TREE
Melaleuca styphelioides	PRICKLY MELALEUCA
Pinus canariensis	CANARY ISLAND PINE
Pseutosuga menziesii	DOUGLAS FIR
Quercus ilex	HOLLY OAK
Sequoia sempervirens	COAST REDWOOD
Ulmus parvifolia	CHINESE or EVERGREEN ELM

LOVING CARE OF OLD OAK TREES

Los Altos is blessed with a large number of very big old oak trees. Unfortunately, building, paving and landscaping near these trees can easily damage their root systems and hasten their demise. If you own one of these magnificent oaks, it is important to understand their water needs and their root systems. Oaks have a number of deep roots to support their huge size, but the bulk of the feeder roots, which take up moisture and nutrients, are located in the top 1-3 feet of soil and extend as much as 90 feet out beyond the drip line. These roots are adapted to being wet in cool weather and dry in warm weather. If the soil gets compacted or dug into, or if extra soil is added on top of the existing soil level, the roots become damaged and the tree cannot fight off infection or starvation.

To keep oaks healthy
- Do not water near mature oaks in the summer. Young oaks will need some water year round.
- Plant only drought tolerant California native shrubs and groundcovers within the root protection zone (RPZ), which is half again as big as the area between the trunk and the drip line. Do not plant within 6 feet of the trunk. Limit the amount of digging you do in this area.
- Do not put extra soil on top of the RPZ or compact the soil in any way.
- Leave fallen leaf litter in place to act as a mulch.
- Provide adequate drainage around the tree. Basements and swimming pools that are down slope from oaks can act as dams, leaving oak roots too wet.
- Put all utilities in one trench, preferably bored 3 feet underground to avoid destroying feeder roots.
- Use decking rather than paving near oaks.
- Consult a certified arborist if the tree looks stressed or unhealthy or if you plan to do some home improvements that might impact it.
- To prevent Sudden Oak Death Syndrome, don't bring in plants that are possible carriers, don't bring in fire wood from contaminated areas, and wash tires, boots and tools before leaving any contaminated areas.

There are three major diseases of which you should be aware. Two, crown rot and oak root fungus, are most often caused by frequent summer watering or damage to the tree's roots. Symptoms include yellowing and thinning of leaves, dieback of twigs, and general malaise. Crown rot also causes oozing of dark colored fluid from lesions in the bark. Oak root fungus is characterized by white filaments in the soil and mushrooms. The third disease is Sudden Oak Death syndrome caused by the Phytophthora pathogen, a new problem in north/central California. It is characterized by dark red to tar-black thick sap oozing on the bark surface. This bleeding is typically found between the root crown (the area where the trunk fans out to the roots) and a height of 6 feet. If your tree develops any of these symptoms, consult an arborist immediately. Sometimes the tree can be saved.

For more information see the website of the California Oak Foundation: ***http://www.californiaoaks.org***. For information about Sudden Oak Death Syndrome seethe website for University of California Cooperative Extension in Marin County: ***http://cemarin.ucdavis.edu/symptoms.html***.

A CALENDAR OF TREES WITH FLOWERS OR BRIGHT COLORED LEAVES

JANUARY/FEBRUARY

Acacia baileyana—yellow flowers
Acer palmatum 'Sango Kaku'—bright red bark
Eucalyptus sideroxylon—clusters of puffy pink flowers
Magnolia (deciduous)—large pink, maroon or white flowers
Prunus (almond)—pink flowers
Prunus cerasifera—pink flowers, purple leaves
Pyrus kawakamii—white flowers

MARCH/APRIL

Acacia melanoxylon—creamy white flowers
Aesculus x carnea—bright red or pink flower clusters
Arbutus menziesii—white bell-shaped flowers
Cercis canadensis—small pink or white sweet-pea shaped flowers
Cercis occidentalis—small magenta sweet-pea shaped flowers
Cornus florida—white or pink 2" flower bracts
Eriobotrya deflexa—clusters of white flowers
Eriobotrya japonica—orange fruit in clusters
Leptospermum laevigatum—white flowers
Magnolia grandiflora—huge white flowers
Malus (crabapple)—pink flowers
Melaleuca—masses of fuzzy white flower clusters
Prunus (plum)—white flowers
Prunus (apricot)—white flowers with red centers
Prunus (flowering cherry)—white to dark pink flowers
Pyrus calleryana—white flowers
Robinia x ambigua 'Idahoensis'—red-violet flower clusters

Robinia x ambigua 'Descaisneana'—pink flower clusters
Tamarix—tiny pink flowers
Tristania laurina—fragrant small yellow flowers

MAY/JUNE

Aesculus californica—white flower spikes
Brachychiton populneus—white bell-shaped flowers
Callisemon—bright red bottle-brush shaped flowers
Castanea dentate—long sprays of small white flowers
Citrus, Valencia Orange—orange fruit
Cornus capitata—masses of 2" creamy flower bracts
Crataegus species—white or pink flower clusters
Dais continifoliaa—pink pompom flowers
Erythrina crista-galli—clusters of bright red flowers
Hymenosporum flavum—yellow flowers
Jacaranda mimosifolia—showy lavender–blue flowers
Koelreuteria paniculata—clusters of yellow flowers
Lyonothamnus floribundus asplenifolius—white flowers
Magnolia grandiflora—huge white flowers
Melia—3/4" star shaped lavender flowers
Tilia cordata—small flowers surrounded by 2" white papery bracts

JULY/AUGUST

Ailanthus altissima—rust-colored seed pod clusters
Albizia julibrissin—pink powder-puff flowers
Braheia armata—large hanging clusters of creamy flowers
Butia capitata—long spikes of creamy flowers
Chitalpa x tashkentensis—showy white, pink or lavender flowers

Erythrina crista-galli—clusters of bright red flowers
Eucalyptus ficifolia—clusters of puffy red or orange flowers
Grevillea robusta—sprays of orange flowers
Lagerstroemia indica—white, red pink or purple flowers
Ligustrum lucidum—white flowers
Lophostemon confertus—white flowers
Magnolia grandiflora—huge white flowers

SEPTEMBER/OCTOBER

Diospyros kaki—apricot and orange leaves, orange fruit
Erythrina crista-galli—clusters of bright red flowers
Eriobotrya japonica—dull white flower clusters
Gleditsia triacanthos—yellow fernlike leaves, 12–18" seedpods
Koelreuteria paniculata—red to brown "Chinese Lantern"
    seedpods
Magnolia grandiflora—huge white flowers
Malus (crabapple)—small red fruits
Pseudotsuga macrocarpa—7" cones hanging down
Zelkova serrata—yellow, orange, or dark red leaves

NOVEMBER/DECEMBER

Acer buergeranum—orange/ red leaves
Acer macrophyllum—yellow leaves
Acer palmatum—red leaves
Acer platanoides—yellow leaves
Acer saccharinum—yellow leaves
Alnus rhombifolia—small cones decorate branches
Arbutus menziesii—orange-red berries
Arbutus unedo—white or pink bell–shaped flowers
Cercis canadensis—round yellow leaves

Citrus–Washington Navel orange—orange fruit
Crataegus species—red berries
Ilex aquifolium—red berries
Lagerstroemia indica—Some kinds have red leaves
Liquidambar—red & orange leaves
Liriodendron tulilpifera—yellow leaves
Nyssa sylvatica—yellow & orange leaves turning to red
Parrotia persica—yellow, pink, & bright red leaves
Pistache—brilliant red leaves, clusters of red or black berries
Quercus rubra—orange to brown leaves
Sapium sebiferum—red purple and orange flowers
Schinus molle—clusters of pink berries

Apricot Orchard at City Hall

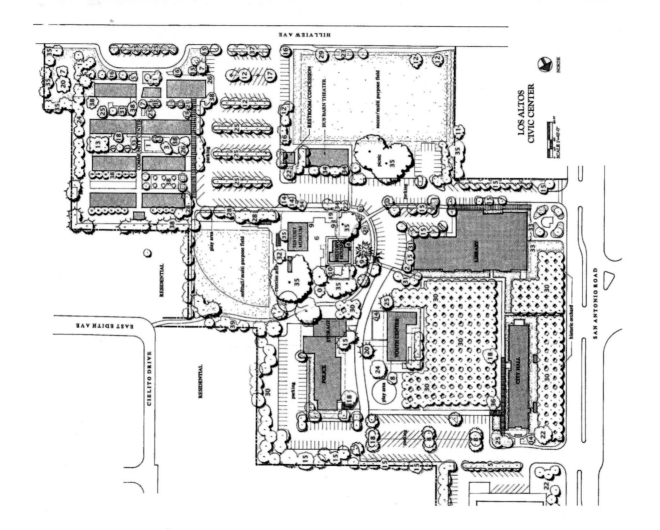

Trees in Los Altos Civic Center

Key to Numbers on Map

0   Acer macrophyllum   Maple, Big Leaf
1   Acer palmatum   Maple, Japanese
2   Araucaria excelsa   Norfolk Island Pine
3   Alnus rhombifolia   White Alder
4   Arbutus unedo   Strawberry Tree
5   Betula pendula   Birch, White
6   Cercis occidentalis   Western Redbud
7   Cedrus deodara   Deodar Cedar
8   Cinnamomun camphora   Camphor
9   Crataegus laevigata   English Hawthorne
10   Erythrina crista-galli   Coral Tree
11   Eucalyptus   Eucalyptus
12   Fraxinus velutina 'Modesto'   Modesto Ash
13   Gleditsia triacanthos   Honey Locust
14   Lagerstroemia indica   Crape Myrtle
15   Liquidambar styraciflua   Liquidambar
16   Liriodendron tulipifera   Tulip Tree
17   Lyonothamnus asplenifolius   Catalina Ironwood
18   Magnolia grandiflora   Magnolia, Southern
19   Maytenus boaria   Mayten Tree
20   Morus alba   Mulberry, fruitless
21   Myoporum laetum   Myoporum
22   Olea europaea   Olive
23   Pinus canariensis   Pine, Canary Island
24   Pinus radiata   Pine, Monterey
25   Pistacia chinensis   Chinese Pistache
26   Pittisporum undulatum   Victorian Box
27   Phoenix canariensis   Canary Island Date Palm
28   Platanus x acerifolia   London Plane Tree
29   Populus fremonti   Cottonwood Poplar
30   Prunus armeniaca   Apricot
31   Prunus cerasifera 'Thundercloud'   Purple Leaf Plum 'Thundercloud'
32   Prunus dulcis   Almond
33   Prunus serrulata   Cherry, flowering
34   Pyrus calleryana 'Chanticleer'   Flowering Pear 'Chanticleer'
35   Quercus agrifolia   Oak, Live
36   Quercus lobata   Oak, Valley or White
37   Robinia x ambigua 'Idahoensis'   Idaho Locust
38   Sequoia Sempervirens   Redwood, Coast
39   Schinus molle   California Pepper Tree

Coast Live Oak